Waiting for Wrigley

Paul Joseph Sullivan

Wide Mouth Bass Publications

Wide Mouth Bass Publications
www.waitingforwrigley.com

Waiting for Wrigley
Paul J. Sullivan

Copyright 2014 © Paul Sullivan

Cover Photos and Design: Ian Robinson

Interior artwork: www.Depositphotos.com

Printing History:
POD printing October 2014
E-format October 2014

All Rights Reserved. No part of this publication may be reproduced in any form without prior written permission from the author.

ISBN-13: 978-0692272060 (Wide Mouth Bass Publications)
ISBN-10: 0692272062

Acknowledgments

Because I'll most likely never win an Academy Award, the list of folks who helped me along the way will be recognized here, without the threat of being cut out by music starting to play or a commercial. Many people played important roles helping us save our Great Dane puppy. Without the help and skill of the vets, their staffs, many specialists and surgeons, Wrigley would not have survived once, let alone three times. There are too many people to thank individually that touched our hearts and made all the difference with Wrigley repeatedly beating the odds against him.

Ultimately, we believe love, ours and many other people's, was the reason Wrigley overcame the medical challenges that threatened to end his life. It was the love and passion to help animals and their families that allowed us to face each ordeal with Wrigley. These folks stand-out: Dr. Shiller, Dr. Knoeckel, Dr. Blumenthal and Dr. McIntyre, but many more impacted our lives with their concern and passion to help Wrigley. We thank you all.

Our families, friends, coworkers and neighbors all supported us, even though at times we know they thought we'd lost our way in our pursuits. Roger, at the Middleburg Equine Swim Center and our neighbor Robin, Wrigley's "second mom," have been wonderful to Wrigley and us, too. The Brahms, the Degens and Brian and Cathy in Kitty Hawk opened their homes to me while I was writing this book. I've also appreciated the concern and stories many people have shared with us about their beloved pets. The kindness we received has been greatly appreciated.

I had help from the very start writing this book from my sister J.S. Sullivan, a technical writer and editor. Also, Don Shalhoub, Patricia Treffinger and Celia Lupo suffered through my early drafts and gave me freely their time and help. My high school buddy, Steve Reagan, also helped by loaning me his mantra, "Stay true to the narrative." The Amill family, Bob Parr and Fadi Abuhamdeh also helped me at important times during my writing.

Karen Cantwell, an accomplished author and family friend, was especially kind in sharing her knowledge of the writing world. She also introduced me to Judy Faldo, who helped me redirect my approach to the writing of *Waiting for Wrigley*. She introduced me to my editor, Maria Schneider. Maria taught me early on why a keyboard has a "delete" button. Maria went far beyond the role of an editor for me. She offered me guidance, support, and honesty in a straightforward and kind manner. With her expertise, *Waiting for Wrigley* evolved into something much more than simply another story about a dog.

Marc Hafkin, PhD, met a confused, self-destructive young man over thirty years ago. The patience, kindness, skill and wisdom he shared with me offered the insight, awareness and emotional strength I needed to choose a different path and celebrate my life with a sense of discovery, playfulness, meaning, integrity and love. Forever thankful.

Without a silly, funny, peculiar, adorable and loving puppy named Wrigley, this story never would have happened. If people come into our lives for reasons, why can't animals play the same role? Our proud Great Dane puppy changed our lives and who we are, simply by being himself. I thank God for Wrigley joining our family. The comfort and happiness I've enjoyed with Wrigley lying behind me, sleeping, snoring and reminding me when it's time for a walk while writing this book has been a wonderful gift and blessing.

Read the book and you'll understand how my life changed when I met my wife, Lisa. If you met her, you would think she was shy and quiet. If you lived with us, you wouldn't think that anymore. My wife is a private person. In the book I've shared intimate moments of our pain, sadness, joy and celebrations. Lisa's willingness and encouragement to share these moments was not easy for her. Her blessing came with the hope that our story of infertility may help others to know broken hearts can be mended and filled with new and different kinds of love and joy. Lisa is my best friend, my sharpest critic and my truest love.

Dedication

To my mother, who supported me in ways I never understood until after she was gone.

Dedication

Chapter 1

Granting Wishes

The boats rocking back and forth in the marina at the city docks in Old Town Alexandria made for a serene setting overlooking the Potomac River. It gave me reason to extend my bench sitting for a little longer. It was peaceful and relaxing until the moment I felt moist, hot air against the back of my neck. I jumped off the bench, arms up and fists clenched, ready to defend myself.

"Do forgive me, sir. A thousand pardons. Patches does forget his manners. I'm sorry we startled you. Do have a pleasant evening." The gentleman's use of the Queen's English made accepting his apology appear to be the proper thing to do.

The old chap resumed his stroll down the cobblestone walkway along the water. Dutifully walking beside him was "Patches," his magnificent Harlequin Great Dane.

I wished the man had stopped longer and perhaps offered me an opportunity to meet his dog. I'd seen pictures of Great Danes, but had never been close to one in person, let alone been breathed on by one.

I've been intrigued by the idea of owning a Great Dane ever since. My fascination with Great Danes lasted for twenty years before having one of my own.

At forty-four years old it was embarrassing to be so excited about getting a dog, but after my wife and I moved into our new house in suburban northern Virginia, the time felt right.

From the upper deck of our new home, I gazed out at the lake. The oak trees in our backyard had to be close to ninety feet tall. It was a magnificent view, especially that night, with the light from the full moon sparkling off the water. I'd met the neighbors two doors up, but couldn't remember their names. I did, however, remember their dog was named Charlie. He was a non-stop barking machine and was presently the only distraction from the beautiful evening. Charlie was incredibly annoying, especially considering his meager size. I hoped our puppy would have better manners. We'd find out soon enough.

My wife, Lisa, and I were scheduled to meet with the breeder Monday night. I'd never met Don in person, but we'd talked several times regarding the puppy we had picked out seven weeks earlier from photographs. In conversations with Don, I had discovered he wasn't a professional breeder. His wife of forty-two years, now deceased, was the trained, certified breeder in the family. Breast cancer took her life two years earlier. Breeding Great Danes was Don's wife's passion, not his. But he continued the business in respect and honor of her. He was retired military, working for a defense contractor in Iraq.

While we had planned to meet on Monday, Don called while I was relaxing on the back deck. "My itinerary's changed. I have to leave for Iraq earlier than expected. I know it's late notice, but is it possible for you to pick him up tonight?"

It was already eight-thirty PM, but I didn't hesitate answering. "Absolutely. We can meet tonight. No problem." The phone call ended just as Lisa walked outside for some fresh air. I hadn't checked with her about the sudden change in the pickup time, confident she wouldn't mind.

"That was Don?" she asked. "What did he want? Nothing's wrong with the puppy is there? Everything is still on for tomorrow, right?"

Lisa's habit of asking several questions in a row demonstrates how her mind works. She is a nurse practitioner. Quick, factual answers help her save lives. My accuracy in answering what she considered the most important question first had improved over the five years we'd been married.

"The puppy's fine. Don can't meet tomorrow. He wants to meet *next* Sunday," I said.

"Next Sunday? The puppy will be nine weeks old by then! We'll miss an entire week of his prime puppy cuteness stage. Call back and tell Don we'll drive to his farm and pick the puppy up tonight. Paul, I'm not waiting another week. You agreed to that without asking me? I can't believe you sometimes."

"Did I say *next* Sunday?" I asked. "I meant *this* Sunday, as in two hours."

"Paul! Tell me the truth. And I don't think you're one bit funny," she informed me. I wasn't sure if she was sincerely annoyed with me or trying to hold back her excitement about getting the puppy a day early.

"No joke. He wants to meet tonight at ten-thirty. He's flying out of Andrews Air Force Base tomorrow at five in the morning heading back to Iraq. Aren't you psyched? We're going to have our puppy tonight!" I felt bad for teasing her because I would have been as disappointed as she was over the thought of waiting. It was a nice change having something we were both excited about and looking forward to. Lisa wanted to leave immediately, but we waited until nine to avoid sitting in the parking lot. I drove fifteen miles an hour over the speed limit most of the way, so we still ended up waiting.

The rendezvous was at the WaWa Gas & Shop Stop, just off Rt. 50, three miles past the Bay Bridge, just over the Maryland state line.

Even though Don told us he'd be driving a white Ford pickup truck, we inspected every single truck that pulled into the lot, no matter the color. At ten thirty-five, an older model white Ford pickup truck drove past the gas pumps by the entrance to the store and parked on the far side of the building under a bright light.

A gray haired gentleman got out of the vehicle, went around to the passenger side and opened the door. He came back around with a small black and white puppy nestled tightly in his arms.

We stared at the puppy, while the man peered around the lot.

My dream was about to become a reality. I had no idea how this puppy was going to change our lives. My wise Grandma often preached, "Be careful what you ask for."

Opening my door, I said, "What are we waiting for, Lisa? That's him. Let's go."

"You sure?" she asked, already five steps ahead of me and practically running.

"It'd be a hell of a coincidence, don't you think? Slow down!" I tried catching up, but Lisa had the puppy in her arms by the time I arrived at the white truck.

"Oh, my God. You're the cutest little thing I've ever laid eyes on," she said, raising the puppy into the air. "Look at him, Paul. He's even cuter in person."

The puppy was a Mantle Great Dane. Breeders sought them out because of their markings' popularity with buyers. Our puppy's jet-black markings contrasted with his pure white fur. He was white from a sharp point between his eyes and down around his nose and mouth. The white fur continued beneath his snout, covering his chest like a bib, and wrapped around his chest, almost tying off like a scarf around his neck. The two inches at the end of his long tail looked as though it had been dipped into a bucket of white paint. All four of his paws were brilliant white, forming adorable boots. His paws appeared to belong on another, much larger animal.

Because this puppy's white fur didn't make it completely around his neck, he was considered an "imperfect" Mantle. We assumed this slight color deviation was the reason he was picked last from his litter. It didn't bother me or Lisa, because we had no plans for breeding or showing our dog.

The puppy was perfect; everything I wanted. The little guy had already grown from the picture we'd seen when he was only a week old. He was now eight weeks old and twelve pounds. His head was ridiculously large in proportion to his small body. Equally ungainly and large were his floppy ears, which hung down the sides of his fat face almost touching his paws.

Lisa set the puppy down on the pavement. He ran to Don, jumping up on his leg, falling and rolling back on his side. He was literally tripping over himself, the proverbial "two left feet." We couldn't stop laughing, watching him bumble around, falling over.

While Don and I completed the paperwork, Lisa carried the puppy to a grassy area close to where we'd parked. She knelt at first, but ended up rolling on the ground with the puppy within a minute. He jumped up, trying to climb on her and kept falling off.

"You're so cute, I can't stand it!" She talked to him in the same pitch she normally used with babies and toddlers.

I was spellbound as I watched them play. Don noticed my longing and wrapped things up. He finished by telling me something that took on greater meaning for Lisa and me at a later time.

"You know your pup was the runt of the litter, don't you?" He lowered his voice, as if he was confiding a national secret.

"There's always a runt. It doesn't mean anything long term, usually. But they get pushed around. Some are ignored by their mothers. The more dominant pups pick on them too. It's normal, instinctive pack behavior. Most animals in the wild identify the weak in their pack and run them off. He's coming along nicely though, your pup. You need to be patient with him, because he gets frazzled pretty easily. You'll see what I mean soon enough. I'm sure he'll be fine once he's settled down," he told me.

It sounded like information I didn't need, and I wasn't clear why he'd shared it with me. But I thanked him for everything and we shook hands, saying goodbye.

Lisa waited for me outside the SUV, handing the puppy to me when I walked up. It was my first opportunity to hold him. We looked at each other. He licked my chin. Then he farted into my hands.

I said, "Nice greeting," and handed him back to Lisa.

She smiled. "You two already have something in common."

"Bravo. Very funny, Lisa." I watched her set the puppy back down and smell her hands.

"You know what I think, Paul? I'm in love. I'm in love with you, and I'm in love with our beautiful puppy. He's so cute." She picked him back up and squeezed him close.

The muscles in my face hurt from smiling. We could have played in the parking lot with the puppy for another hour, but a long drive home awaited us, and it was almost eleven o'clock.

I asked Lisa, "Should we put him in the crate for the drive home?"

"Are you serious? He's staying here with me. We need to get to know each other. I work tomorrow, remember? This is the only time I have with this little fella until tomorrow night. It's not fair. I'm jealous you'll get him all to yourself." Lisa set the puppy on her lap after getting into the Yukon and held him, making sure he didn't roll off.

"You may want to support his head. He's definitely going down face first if he falls," I warned.

"That's not nice. Puppies have awkward growing stages, kind of like your belly." She glanced at me slyly, assessing how I was taking her insult. "Seriously Paul, stop making fun of him or he'll get a complex." She covered his floppy ears, pretending to shield the puppy from my insensitive observations.

Fifteen minutes into our drive home the puppy fell asleep on Lisa's lap. She was bummed because she wanted to play with him. When we crossed the Bay Bridge, the puppy was awakened by the humming of the tires, giving Lisa another chance to play with him.

Lisa asked, "What did Don have to say?"

Before I could answer, she began talking to the puppy.

"You're the cutest little bug, aren't you?" She pinched the loose skin around the little guy's face. My grandmother used to do stuff like that to me. I hated it. The worst was when she used her own spit to flatten my cowlick.

Lisa pushed her face into the puppy's, then pulled away. "It feels like we waited forever to get you, fella. I'm glad you're finally here." She kissed his cold, little black nose, looked over at me, and said, "I love him already. It's weird, it feels like he's been with us a long time."

It was freaky because she described how I was feeling exactly. Once we passed Annapolis, Lisa and the puppy were both asleep. I kept the radio off and thought about what Lisa had said about waiting forever. We had waited a long time. I'm not convinced the wait time was about the puppy entirely. The first five years of our marriage, Lisa and I had waited for something that we couldn't have: a baby of our own. It sounds insignificant to compare getting a puppy to having a baby, but this was the closest we'd come to reaching the goal. This puppy was real, not a hope or wish. He was alive and asleep in Lisa's arms.

Our road to this point had been hard. We'd tried artificial insemination six times, followed by four in vitro fertilization cycles. We never got pregnant; not even close. The process almost ended our marriage. Thankfully, our marriage counselor helped us come to terms with our infertility. We'd done our best to put it behind us, but I knew not all the sadness or disappointment had completely disappeared. At least it hadn't for me. But in that moment, driving home with my wife and new puppy I believed, for the first time in a long time, that we could be happy again, maybe even as happy as we were before we started trying to have a family of our own.

Driving home that night was a special time for me. I found a new hope that maybe Lisa and I could find what we had lost.

We pulled into our driveway at half past midnight. Lisa woke up, as did the puppy, as soon as I cut the engine off.

"Thanks for driving, sweetie. When did I fall asleep? Don't you think the puppy should sleep with us tonight?" she asked me.

"Annapolis," I said.

"What are you talking about?" she asked.

I'd picked the wrong question to answer, but I was sleepy and my guessing game was off.

"He should sleep with us tonight. I don't want him to be alone his first night. Just tonight, please. We'll crate him starting tomorrow," she promised.

This was new. Lisa had just answered her own questions. She already knew how I felt about the dog sleeping with us. Knowing I was going to object, she offered a caveat, sounding like a compromise. Tomorrow night she'd say, "It's a transition period. He should sleep with us for the rest of the week until he's comfortable in the house. I swear, then we'll crate him." I could already hear her.

I usually caved when Lisa pressed for something. Our marriage counselor suggested I ask more firmly for things I wanted. She was probably correct. I wanted to make Lisa happy, but more than that, I agreed because I didn't want to deal with her disappointment. I'd never considered myself a "people-pleaser," but it was difficult to ignore how often I acquiesced to her wishes.

The puppy needed crating for his safety no matter where he slept. There were three possible problem areas awaiting him inside. Lisa and I didn't live alone; we shared our home with three cats. Mr. Precious was a twelve-year-old, long-haired Himalayan. Miss Cassie was a thirteen-year-old, rare Ocicat. Finally, there was Zoe, seventeen years old, and affectionately referred to as "the little bitch."

Precious and Cassie were indoor cats and had never been exposed to dogs. Zoe was an indoor/outdoor cat. Her limited experiences with dogs always ended with her running for her life or climbing a tree for safety.

Lisa, an excellent researcher, had gathered information about introducing a new pet into a home with existing animals. She couldn't find any specific literature regarding blending three old cats with a new puppy. That may have been the most telling information in and of itself. In general, most of the literature suggested separating the pets at first, then slowly increasing their time together under supervision. Blissful cohabitation was the end goal.

None of the research took into account my penchant for immediate gratification. I'm not ashamed to admit immediate gratification is the driving force behind many of my decisions.

"Do you *really* want to do all that separation stuff with the puppy and the cats?"

"It's probably a good idea. The puppy can barely get around on his own feet. I'm afraid when Zoe attacks him he won't be able to get away."

"When she attacks him? Come on, have some faith," I said, despite knowing Zoe would try to teach the puppy who was boss first thing.

Zoe was called "the little bitch" for a good reason. After we brought Cassie home, six months passed before she'd dare to stray beyond our bedroom doorway. Zoe would patrol the stairs, challenging Cassie to come down. Zoe never weighed more than seven pounds, but she was all business when it came to her territory. At seventeen years old, she hunted mice and birds and still intimidated cats twice her size. She was sweet with humans, but Zoe never sought out other animals' companionship.

Precious was part of a package deal. He came with Lisa when we married. He was determined to keep me from stealing Lisa from him while we were dating. My overnights at Lisa's condo were met with stinky piles of cat poop on my side of the bed.

When that didn't work, his second assault came in the form of gas released from his butt into my face once my head hit the pillow.

Constantly changing his strategies, he started waiting until I fell asleep, which provided him the timing and position to achieve perfect aim. That tactic did, however, increase his chances of being choked to death if I woke up. He counted on Lisa to rescue him, which she did on several occasions. When those attempts failed to push me out the door, I could always count on my overnight bag being soaked in cat urine the following morning. It was his feline means test, gauging how much I loved Lisa.

I passed the test only after giving her a ring. I'd often wondered how many before me had failed Precious' litmus test of love.

Cassie belonged to my dad's second wife. After their divorce, she headed back to Canada, leaving him and the cat behind. Cassie was the most beautiful silver and gray cat Lisa and I had ever come across. Her friendship, leading to a strong alliance with Precious, helped stop Zoe's rude behavior, but it was a full year before we had peace after Cassie's arrival.

We were confident Zoe wouldn't react particularly well to the puppy, but were unsure how Cassie and Precious would take the news.

"What time is it?" Lisa asked as we sat motionless in the Yukon trying to decide what to do with the pup.

"Almost one in the morning."

"I'm wiped out. Let's just take him in and see what happens. We can do all those things I read about tomorrow if things get out of control," she said.

"Sounds reasonable to me." Who was I to argue with such a simple plan?

Moments like that reminded me of why I wanted to marry Lisa. I knew she was smart when we met, but I'd learned she was pragmatic and able to make quick decisions without second guessing.

Lisa set the puppy down on the front lawn. While she waited for him to pee, I opened the breezeway door into the kitchen and turned on the light. Lisa followed behind, carrying the puppy.

Zoe tried to run out before the door shut, but Lisa stopped her by sticking her foot out and re-routing the cat towards the dining room. We kept her inside at night because of prowling foxes and other predators.

Precious was perched on top of the cushion of his favorite chair in the living room. Cassie came down from upstairs when she heard us come in.

"Well, no time like the present," I said, aware that all the cats were staring at the small puppy in Lisa's arms.

There was an archetypal caveman curiosity inside of me. It was balanced with a sincere concern for the puppy. This was likely the closest I'd get to watching the Romans throw a Christian into the lion's den. I don't think Lisa shared my intrigue.

"This is your new family, little guy. Precious, Cassie, Zoe, this is…our new puppy." Lisa set him down in the center of the living room. "We really need to name him. Puppy will not fly forever."

The puppy began bopping around the room and sniffing everything around him. He stopped when he caught a glimpse of Cassie. She jumped up on a dining room chair, then poked her head out from under the tablecloth. After a few seconds, she'd seen enough.

She jumped down and ran up the stairs, most likely returning to our bedroom to hide behind the dresser.

The puppy looked over at the staircase. Thus distracted, he did not see Precious arch his back high and then reach out with a long stretch before jumping down from his cushion.

The puppy turned and found himself facing the flat-faced Himalayan.

Precious casually walked closer to him, fixing his eyes on the puppy's curious face. Precious confidently turned his back on the tiny Great Dane, carefully walked down the hallway and retreated up the stairs.

Zoe now stood in the doorway of the kitchen that led into the living room. She crept slowly toward the puppy.

He stuck his little black nose in her direction just as she was close enough to touch.

I was shocked. Was Zoe offering an olive branch of friendship?

A second before I could give my best impression of Al Michaels' "Do you believe in miracles?" Zoe started with her right paw. I counted five rapid, successive and successful hits. They all landed and one scraped the unsuspecting puppy's nose.

Poor little fellow didn't have a chance. He tried to escape, but his paws slid out in different directions because of the slippery hardwood floors. Zoe's left paw swung wildly again, but failed to make any serious contact.

Lisa dove in and picked the puppy up. She cradled him close to her chest.

I'm not sure the puppy had figured out what was going on, but he'd met Zoe. Environmental/behavioral puppy/feline home study concluded.

"Poor little guy. You didn't deserve that. Zoe, you're a mean old cat," Lisa said. "It's okay, fella. I've got you." She pressed her face against his.

"That went exactly how I thought it would. You ready to go to bed? I'll get his crate from the car." I headed back outside.

Even though she had brought up keeping the dog with us this first night, I'd made it clear I didn't want the dog sleeping in our bed. Precious and Cassie were already sharing our pillows. A Great Dane needed to know our bed was our bed, not his. Lisa didn't agree, but I was sticking to my guns on this.

Lisa went upstairs while I retrieved the puppy's crate. I placed it in the dining room. Lisa had set out a small blanket for the little guy to sleep on in his crate.

I placed the puppy inside, gave him a goodnight pat and latched the door. He appeared to be doing just fine.

I reached the top of the stairs, almost into our bedroom, when the crying started from inside the crate.

Lisa and I listened for twenty minutes. It was too painful to ignore. Lisa had to be up at four-thirty, only a few hours away, so I went down to check on him.

Every time I walked up to the crate, he'd stop crying and stare at me with his sad puppy eyes. Each time I walked away, he'd cry.

At two o'clock, Lisa woke up. "He finally fell asleep?" she asked.

"Not exactly," I said.

"Paul Sullivan. You are too funny. No dog in the bed, huh? Not even one night, you told me. You're bad." She scooped the puppy up from the bottom of our bed and placed him between us.

I was exhausted, but couldn't fall asleep. I laid in bed waiting for the sun to rise in anticipation of spending an entire day with our new puppy.

Chapter 2

Forming an Identity

"The little guy's still asleep, but he probably needs to go out," Lisa said, kissing me and the puppy good morning and goodbye at the same time. "Maybe you'll think of a good name today. You'll have all day to think about it while you're getting to know him."

Lisa was giving me a hard time already, and the sun wasn't even up yet. We had considered naming the puppy after we picked him out from the photograph. I lobbied to put off making a decision until we met him, wanting to know his personality before naming him. I thought waiting for the introduction was an important part of choosing a fitting name. Lisa reluctantly agreed, but not-so-secretly let me know she thought I was nuts.

Lisa worked in a teaching, not-for-profit hospital in Washington DC. It was an hour away with light traffic. I wouldn't see her again until eight-thirty that night. She cared for patients after surgery. My wife was smart and an excellent nurse practitioner who genuinely cared about her patients. I respected her commitment, while admiring and envying her for loving her job.

I wasn't as jazzed with my own career choice. I ran a custom paint contracting business. I'd painted houses to pay for college and then graduate school. The jobs provided good money and the hours allowed me to travel in the off-season. My current schedule provided me plenty of freedom during my day. That was one positive aspect of entrepreneurship, but I'd been doing the same thing for twenty years. Once Lisa and I married, I relied on employees to handle the day-to-day operations. My lack of interest had started to affect my company's bottom line. Worse, I didn't care enough about the problem to start fixing it.

A cold, wet, black nose pressed against my face, waking me again after Lisa had left.

All three cats watched as I walked downstairs with the puppy in my arms. I immediately took him outside. He might be eight weeks old, but he wasn't accustomed to walking in high grass.

I made a mental note to lower the blade on our lawnmower.

He sniffed everything, not moving far from where I'd set him down. He completed his business, number one and two, quickly.

"Good job, buddy," I said, purposely extending my vowel sounds, hoping he'd understand that getting his business done quickly warranted high praise.

Lisa's earlier point was well taken. We needed to give him a name sooner rather then later. I consider naming him "Goofy," but wasn't convinced it was completely accurate or fair.

Four days passed without us being able to agree upon a name. Lisa had Friday off, so we designated it D-Day: dog-naming day.

Greek God references were out. There were too many Apollo and Zeus Great Danes out there already. We both wanted a friendly name to help ease people's anxiety, because we had no doubt our puppy was going to become a large dog.

Great Danes are referred to as "Gentle Giants" because of their relaxed and amicable personalities, but they can still be intimidating, especially for those unfamiliar with the breed.

It surprised us that we couldn't find a name we both liked quickly. Lisa's mom suggested we call the pup "No-name." After printing out a list of puppy names from several websites we knew we weren't the only folks struggling with the process. After we reached the names starting with the letter "V" without an agreement, Lisa and I became more discouraged.

The puppy rested against Lisa on the couch while we scrolled down the shrinking list of potential names. He'd occasionally look up when Lisa repeated a certain name, but we didn't like the ones he responded to until hitting the "W's."

Lisa read down the list, "Woofy, Worton, Wregan, Wrigley."

She stopped.

"Wrigley. Wrigley? WRIGLEY!" she shouted. The puppy jumped up. Certainly, this time it was his sign of approval! Okay, most likely he was reacting to Lisa's excitement, but we ran with it, taking it as a sign of his enthusiasm and acceptance.

We both repeated the name like it was our mantra. "Wrigley, Wrigley, Wrigley."

"It reminds me of Wrigley Field," I said, having been born outside of Chicago. "The name gives me a happy feeling, just like him. Wrigley Sullivan. Mr. Wrigley. Puppy Wrigley. Hmmm, what do you think, Lisa? Agreed?"

She leaned over, hauling the puppy onto her lap. "Mr. Wrigley Sullivan. It's official. You're the most handsome puppy in the world. And from this point on, you'll be recognized as Puppy Wrigley. Do you like it, fella?" She pressed her nose into his.

The way she acted, I think she was expecting him to answer.

Wrigley turned around and rolled off her lap onto the cushion. "He's completely bowled over by it!" She laughed with delight and then picked up a pen and paper. She wrote 'Wrigley' and then added 'Sullivan' after it. She had done the same thing with her own name after getting engaged.

I loved this fun side of her. It was a glimpse of why I enjoyed being with her.

"Your name looks cute too, just like you," she said, hugging Wrigley. "Now we can take you to the vet. Imagine what they'd think of us showing up without a name for you! By the way, Paul," she said with a smile for me, "his appointment is at two o'clock tomorrow afternoon in case you've forgotten, and I'll bet you twenty bucks you did."

I had forgotten. But the vet trip would be okay, because I liked taking Wrigley anywhere. I loved watching people react to him. They'd stop, ask what kind of dog he was, comment on the size of his paws, and then start speculating on how big he was going to grow.

Instinctively, people wanted to pick him up, sometimes without asking, which bothered me. Wrigley welcomed the attention most of the time, but he didn't like chaotic activity. If there were more than two people, he'd hide behind or between my legs, waiting for me to pick him up. He hated loud noises too. He'd freeze, like in a cartoon when a boulder falls from the sky and there is no escape from being hit.

Wrigley and I became constant companions. He loved traveling. I'd say the word "ride" and he'd meet me at the breezeway door if he wasn't already there after hearing my keys.

I'd load him in the passenger seat next to me. He'd sit and watch me drive or curl up and take a nap. I'm not sure why, but he had no interest in looking out the window. He didn't mind being left alone for short periods, either. I'd run into the store or check on a job and find him fast asleep when I returned. My customers enjoyed meeting him, and I loved introducing him. Wrigley made routine errands fun and time fly by. Our puppy filled my day with welcome, entertaining distractions.

Our neighborhood was small, only ninety-nine homes. Lisa and I met more neighbors in one weekend walking Wrigley than the entire month we had lived there before his arrival. We were known as, "The new people with the Great Dane puppy."

Wrigley was a rock star in the neighborhood. People claimed they stopped by to meet us, but they'd bring their pets or young kids and always managed to ask if they could meet Wrigley.

Cat people didn't seem to gravitate to each other like dog people. Dog people always enjoy watching their dog greet other dogs, even when that included the circular smelling of the butts ritual. Not only did Wrigley make plenty of friends in no time, we met some great folks too.

It was impossible to hold back our laughter when Wrigley jumped and rolled around trying to gain his footing while playing with other dogs. There was a dog in our neighborhood known for his aggression. Wrigley played with the infamous pup without any problem. It wasn't rational, but I was proud to be Wrigley's owner.

A neighbor told Lisa how her husband never liked dogs, but he admitted if they could find one like Wrigley, he'd consider getting one. That was before he realized Wrigley was only twelve weeks old and a Great Dane, destined to become a huge dog.

Wrigley was growing up fast, but continued his "awkward" growing stage as Lisa affectionately labeled it. The latest physical attribute to add to the list was his left ear standing completely straight up while his other ear remained flopped down. He looked as though he was straining to hear something far, far away.

It took three weeks before the independent ear relaxed and fell back down. That was just Wrigley. Things worked differently with him.

Most nights, an hour after Wrigley ate his dinner, I'd take him on a walk around the lake. We never completed the entire route because Wrigley was too busy chasing leaves and smelling everything along the way. He'd also tire quickly. Lisa joined us when she was home, but even when she couldn't come along, the walk was something I looked forward to, and I think he did too.

Wrigley hung out in his crate sometimes, even though it was almost too small for him already. I think it was his dog-cave, a fortress away from the unpredictable Zoe. Most of the rest of his time he spent on the living room sofa.

Every night, I found myself looking forward to taking him outside before Lisa and I went to bed. That said, one of us usually had to get up at two or three in the morning to let him out to pee. It disrupted our sleep, but we wanted a house-trained dog from the start.

The cats gradually accepted having Wrigley as part of our family. Even Zoe became disinterested in beating him up over time. Her ignoring Wrigley may have had more to do with his increased size than disinterest, but that didn't matter. Our home was calm and at peace in a way that it hadn't been since our realization that we couldn't have children. There was no doubt in my mind we were a stronger couple because of the baby issue, but we got married because we wanted a family. There was a feeling of failure and of being victims associated with infertility. We'd always achieved what we set out to do up until then. It was a painful bond to share.

Our marriage counseling helped deal with the loss, but I don't think we'd recaptured that feeling of ease we shared before it all started. Wrigley was helping bring laughter and joy back into our lives. We were feeling happy again. That gave me hope.

Chapter 3

Stop Doing That!

Lisa, Wrigley and I arrived at the vet's office twenty minutes early. Dr. Shiller's clinic was a one-man show. It wasn't unusual for appointments to be running behind. We didn't mind waiting because it gave us an opportunity to show off Wrigley.

When it was finally our turn, Dr. Shiller greeted us with a big smile. "So this is the new pup? How are the cats getting along with him? Or should I just ask about Zoe?" He laughed. Our vet was well aware of Zoe's unique personality.

One reason we liked Dr. Shiller was because he knew our animals personally. He never rushed our appointments with the animals and wasn't quick to suggest drawing blood for lab analysis or prescribe expensive medications. His fees were sometimes half of what we paid at the large veterinary clinic we used to visit.

Wrigley stared at me while the vet examined him.

Dr. Shiller quickly identified the only thing Lisa and I had noticed amiss.

"In layman terms it's called 'Cherry Eye,'" he explained. "The actual medical word is entropion. His lower lashes are growing at an angle toward his eyes, not outward. Most puppies grow out of it, and this boy's got a lot more growing to do. We'll take a wait and see approach." He laughed at his own pun and gave us ointment for Wrigley's eyes to help reduce the irritation from the rubbing.

There was an effective surgical procedure to correct the condition if it didn't clear up on its own. I always thought it was odd when people chose to have their pets go through surgery. I'd even read an article about a dog on chemotherapy. It seemed crazy to me, but who was I to judge? At twelve weeks, Wrigley was a healthy puppy weighing in at twenty-four pounds and growing fast. Before we left we scheduled another appointment for Wrigley's second round of vaccine shots due in two weeks.

Later during that same week, as I was leaving the house to do a painting estimate, Wrigley heard my keys rattling. He jumped off the sofa and met me at the breezeway door.

He was too big and rambunctious to stay with me in the front seat of the Yukon. I'd lowered all the seats in the back of the SUV and placed Wrigley's new foam cushioned dog bed there. I covered it with an old down comforter for extra padding.

Hell, I would've been happy taking a nap back there, but initially Wrigley protested his new traveling accommodations. He whined and whimpered as though he couldn't see me in the front seat. I talked and cajoled him that first trip. Luckily, he adjusted quickly and by the end of the ride he was relaxing in his new open space as though it was his sofa at home. The only difference was this one had wheels, and I drove him around on it. I felt fortunate Wrigley was an easy rider.

In what seemed like a past life, I used to meet with friends for lunch or drinks once or twice a week when Lisa was working, but it had been three months since I'd met up with anyone. I didn't want to be apart from Wrigley or leave him alone for too long.

Lisa felt the same way. We both preferred to spend time at home in the new house with Wrigley and the cats. I never thought it could happen to us, but we became enthusiastic homebodies. Thanksgiving was a few weeks away, and we were looking forward to spending the first holiday in our new place.

Wrigley's second vet appointment was on Saturday, November 10th. Dr. Shiller reexamined Wrigley's eyes. The ointment was helping reduce the irritation, but his lashes were not correcting themselves with time. Wrigley had gained eight pounds and now weighed thirty-two pounds at fourteen weeks. His second round of shots included a distemper vaccine. Dr. Shiller selected a spot just above Wrigley's left rear leg and injected the vaccine.

"You may notice he's a little lethargic or has a suppressed appetite. Any symptoms are usually mild, if he has any at all. Just in case, keep an eye on him for twenty-four hours," Dr. Shiller said, concluding the appointment.

When we arrived back home, I went outside to catch up on some overdue raking. I filled a tarp full of leaves. When I started pulling it toward the woods Wrigley popped out of the pile. Lisa had put him in there when I'd turned around.

"I thought he'd like the free ride into the woods," she said, trying to pick him up.

Wrigley jumped around and bit the leaves. He charged face first into the pile and popped out on the other side. He could act like such a nut.

"I'm trying to get some work done here," I protested.

As Lisa and Wrigley walked away, I heard her telling him, "Don't take it personally little bug, he chases me away sometimes too."

We used our fireplace for the first time that night. I used half the Sunday edition of the Washington Post to get the kindling lit. I reminisced about the ease of lighting our gas logs at the old condo with only the flip of a switch. When the flames built up and the wood started crackling, I had no doubts my efforts were worth it. We loved the smell and sound of the oak hardwood burning and popping in the fireplace.

Wrigley stared at the flames and pulled his head back whenever the wood sizzled or popped. Lisa and I finished a bottle of wine and watched our puppy experience his first exposure to fire.

After an hour, he jumped up on what clearly had become "his sofa." Wrigley loved the big cushions and had even more space once the throw pillows were removed. He stretched out without a paw or a single inch of his long tail dangling off.

Sunday morning the obnoxious sound of our small, electric coffee grinder woke me up. I wanted to go back to sleep, but the aroma of coffee brewing motivated me out of bed. I love that smell. The clock on the nightstand indicated that it was already nine-fifteen. I knew opening that second bottle of wine was a mistake.

I went downstairs. Lisa was in the kitchen. Wrigley was on his sofa. I opened the breezeway door and started walking outside to retrieve the paper.

Lisa stopped me in the breezeway because I was only wearing my boxers and a t-shirt. I filled my cup with coffee and went inside the living room to say good morning to Wrigley, while Lisa went out to get the newspaper at the end of the driveway.

Wrigley didn't look up at me when I walked into the room. Come to think of it, he didn't jump off the sofa when I opened the door to get the paper either. I set my coffee down on what else, the coffee table, and walked over to him.

"What's up, buddy? No hello? No good morning? Too much wine?" I asked him one question after the other like Lisa did with me all the time. They say couples eventually start to look and act the same over time. That could be scary for both of us.

Wrigley didn't respond to my voice, and he didn't raise his head when I walked over to him.

Something was wrong. An outline of a stain circled where his body was lying on the cushion.

"Wrigley. Outside! NOW!" I yelled. I couldn't believe he had peed on the sofa.

He lifted his head up when I yelled at him. He tried standing up on the wet cushion, but swayed and lost his balance. If I hadn't grabbed him, he'd have fallen face-first on the hardwood floor.

"Wrigley!" I pushed him back onto the edge of the sofa.

Lisa rushed into the living room, wondering what was happening. She'd never heard me raise my voice at Wrigley until then.

"Why are you yelling at him?" It was her only question for me.

In the short time I turned around to answer her, Wrigley tried getting up again. His legs gave out halfway during his attempt. Before I could stop his fall I heard his jaw hit the table just before his body landed head first in front of the sofa onto the hardwood floor. He didn't let out a sound upon impact.

I moved to help him up and inadvertently knocked my hot coffee over. It crashed on the floor, splashing everywhere.

"Dear God, Paul. What are you doing?" Lisa yelled, rushing towards us.

"I stopped him from falling," I shot back.

"That's not how it looked," she said.

"I was trying to help him, Lisa. What do you think? I decided to throw hot coffee on him after pushing him off the sofa? Christ."

In full nurse mode, Lisa bent down on her knees, ignoring my frustration with her question and immediately assessed Wrigley's condition. He wasn't moving, and he remained lying flat on his left side, exactly where he had fallen.

I shoved the coffee table over, trying to give Lisa more room to examine him.

"He's burning up. Feel him," she said, placing my hand on his head.

"Wrigley! Wrigley!" she commanded. "Here, Wrigley. Look at me."

I imagined it was how she sounded at work, dealing with a patient in distress.

"He's becoming non-responsive, Paul. His eyes aren't focusing. We need to get him to the emergency clinic, stat. He looks bad. He's really sick." Her confident take-charge voice cracked. I knew she was scared.

I didn't ask any questions. The word "sick" meant "extremely serious." That's how Lisa often described a patient's condition prior to their death at her hospital. She always said, "They were really sick."

Wrigley yelped when I lifted his lame body from the floor to carry him to the SUV.

"I'm going to stay in the back. I want to monitor his breathing," Lisa told me, jumping into the Yukon with Wrigley. I snapped my seat belt and hit the gas.

She lay next to Wrigley the entire ride with her hand over his chest and her face next to his, continually saying, "Stay with me boy. Please, stay with me Wrigley."

Chapter 4

Living with Decisions

Wrigley's limp body clutched in my arms alerted the staff that they had a real emergency coming through their doors. Wrigley was taken back immediately. Lisa and I sat down in the waiting area of the animal hospital. My heart pounded.

Lisa held my hand. "What happened?" She was as confused and surprised as I was after finding Wrigley on the couch.

We retraced our evening and the morning too, but couldn't identify anything that stood out as unusual. We were interrupted by the receptionist behind the counter, wanting us to fill out paperwork.

I brought it back, handing it over to Lisa.

"Maybe he ate some fertilizer. I spread it the other day. He could've eaten a clump of it. That tennis ball might have had some on it," I said.

"I think it's something else," Lisa disagreed. "I'm wondering if it's a delayed reaction to his vaccine?"

I had totally forgotten about his appointment with Dr. Shiller the day before. He had warned us that dogs sometimes had reactions. But shit, this wasn't a mild symptom. This was catastrophic. A reaction didn't make sense. Wrigley had played after we got home, and he ate like a champ too. We had taken our nightly walk around the lake, and nothing appeared wrong with him.

"Would it take that long for a reaction to occur?" I asked.

"I don't know enough about it," she replied. "When patients in the hospital have negative reactions to medication it usually happens pretty fast. But we know what symptoms to look for in those cases. It's been almost twenty-four hours since the vaccine. That was the time frame Dr. Shiller told us to keep an eye on him."

We deduced the vaccine was the only thing that made sense, but the timing seemed off. One disadvantage of relying on a solo vet like Dr. Shiller was that his clinic was closed on Sunday. Lisa was pretty shaken up and that was out of character. I didn't ask her how bad she thought things were with Wrigley. A part of me already knew, and I didn't want to hear it said out loud.

I noticed a painted red line dividing the waiting room equally. Its purpose was to separate dog owners from sitting next to cat owners. It seemed like a waste of paint to me. There was also a side entrance for owners of "exotic pets." That made more sense. I wouldn't want my dog sitting next to a boa constrictor. I'd spilled my high octane morning caffeine dose all over the living room floor. My thoughts bounced around like a ping pong ball in a lottery wind machine. I needed a Ritalin, which I naturally didn't have with me.

Lisa had advised me to always leave some in my car, but I always forgot. A guy with ADD forgetting to do something, go figure.

I watched the receptionist answer phones, greet customers and check out people when their pets were brought out to go home. I wouldn't kiss my wife in public the way some of these folks laid it on their pets. No wonder the animals needed vaccines.

I half-listened as the receptionist reviewed an invoice with a lady holding a poodle. The dog was wearing an Elizabethan collar. The device, resembling a plastic lampshade, appeared to be suffocating her traumatized pooch. Based on previous experiences with our cats, I concluded those collars caused more anxiety and potential harm to an animal than any good they may provide.

The receptionist read the itemized invoice to the poodle lady. "The extra night of boarding, and the additional medications brings the total to $1846.00. Minus the previous payment on your Visa, your balance is $765.00. Should I put it on the same card?" she asked.

I hadn't considered how much any of this was going to cost. It was an emergency and on a Sunday which meant the fees would be at a premium. I wasn't overly concerned about the money then. I just wanted Wrigley to be better. I imagined he was probably scared. Don, his breeder, was right. Wrigley frazzled easily.

After an hour, a vet came out to speak with us. Lisa and I were calmer than when we'd arrived. The vet's kind and confident manner also helped put us at ease.

We listened intently; she spoke softly.

"Wrigley's a very sick dog," she began. "His temperature was 104.5 when he came back. He's extremely dehydrated. He's having a reaction to something, but we're not certain what it might be. Some of the symptoms point to Lyme disease. He's responding to the IV fluid and his fever has decreased, but it's still elevated. I'm concerned it could spike again. I think it's best if he stays overnight. I'd like to take blood and urine samples. I don't think a definitive diagnosis can be made until we have the lab results."

Lisa asked, "Could the symptoms he's exhibiting be from a negative reaction to a vaccine? Wrigley had his second round of shots yesterday."

"He's not showing classic symptoms for a vaccine reaction," the vet answered. "There's no swelling. Vaccine reactions are accompanied with symptoms similar to anaphylactic shock, and it's almost always immediate. It's possible the shot simply coincided with his current condition. I'm leaning more towards a genetic issue, possibly HOD. His left rear leg is lame," she said.

"The shot was given above his left rear leg," I noted. "He was perfectly healthy yesterday. It's hard to believe there's no connection."

"I know this is difficult. I have a dog and just like you, I'd want to know exactly what was happening to mine. Let me work up a treatment plan and a cost estimate. Take time and decide how you'd like us to move forward. May I have your permission to go ahead with the lab work? That's the most logical place to begin. I think you should plan for him staying overnight," she said as she exited the room.

Lisa and I agreed to go ahead with everything the vet initially suggested, including Wrigley spending the night. The estimated cost was $985.00. There was, however, one more thing we wanted before leaving.

"We'd like to say goodbye to Wrigley," I told the young vet's assistant who handed us Wrigley's collar and copies of the paperwork.

"We also wanted to give him this," Lisa said, taking out Wrigley's favorite stuffed animal, Froggy, from her purse.

It took a few minutes before the girl returned. "I'm sorry. I was asked to tell you it may increase Wrigley's anxiety if he sees you. Pets sometimes become depressed after their owners leave. It's not a good idea right now." She was very sympathetic.

"I understand, but he's never been alone before. We want to say goodbye," I insisted.

We followed the attendant down a long narrow hallway. A line of stacked metal cages lined a wall located in a busy work section of the hospital. It was bright and noisy. I spotted Wrigley in a cage on the second row from the top, third one to the right. An IV bag was hanging outside of his cage. His eyes were shut. His right paw was resting inside a tipped bowl of water. The small blanket covering the bottom of his cage was soaked.

"Hey, Wrigley." I pressed my forehead against the cold metal cage, trying to get as close to him as possible.

His heavy eyes opened a little. He lifted his head a few inches, but he put it down just as quickly.

"You're going to spend the night here, buddy. They're going to help you get better. I'll be here first thing tomorrow morning. Promise." I had a vivid flashback of visiting my mother in the ICU before she died.

"Hi, sweetie. You're a sick little bug, aren't you?" Lisa fought back tears. "I'm sorry for what you're going through, Wrigley." She stuck her finger through the thin metal bars of his cage, gently rubbing his hot black nose.

Lisa turned around. She needed to go, and so did I. I hated seeing him like that.

We left the hospital at two that afternoon. We didn't talk about Wrigley or what had happened on the way home. Going back to say goodbye to Wrigley made both of us queasy.

When we got home, Lisa put her hand in her purse to pull out the house key. She turned to me, holding up Wrigley's little stuffed friend.

"I forgot to leave Froggy," she said.

"He'll see Froggy tomorrow when he's back home," I said confidently.

We waited for a call on Wrigley's progress all afternoon, but it never came.

After the Redskins finished losing another game in the final minutes, Lisa called the emergency animal hospital. She joked that nothing they'd tell us could be as depressing as the end of the game. She was wrong.

Lisa was put on hold for ten minutes before a tech named Megan took her call.

"Sorry for the wait, Mrs. Sullivan. I was getting the vet's latest assessment for Wrigley. I'm afraid his fever spiked again around six-thirty. It peaked at 105 degrees. It's 102 now. He hasn't eaten anything. His condition's been elevated to 'critical.' I'm sorry I don't have better news. Is this the best number to reach you? We may need to contact you later tonight if he doesn't improve," she informed Lisa sadly.

I'd never considered that Wrigley might not get better. Last night he was jumping around and playing in the leaves. Just like that, he might be dying? None of it made sense. Was it possible we might actually lose him?

It's a terrible feeling when events out of your control take hold of your life and only chance, nothing else, decides the outcome.

The first time I was afraid of losing somebody I loved was on September 11, 2001. Lisa was scheduled to fly to Los Angeles that morning. Normally she'd have flown out of Reagan National because it was only two miles from her condo in Old Town Alexandria. I wanted to spend the night with her before she left for her best friend's wedding. I worked to convince her to depart from Dulles Airport, only five miles from my house, instead of flying out of Reagan National. She agreed to stay at my place and had her eye on a non-stop flight to LAX, American Airlines flight 77, leaving at eight-ten in the morning from Dulles.

"Remember the time change," I reminded her. "If Sandy is picking you up at noon, west coast time, you'll be sitting around for a couple hours waiting for her. Take the eleven o'clock flight instead. We'll have more time together in the morning."

She agreed, changing her flight to the later departure time. Unknowingly, that decision changed our lives forever.

We had a great night before she left. In the morning, before taking her to the airport, I went out to pick up some fresh baked bagels for breakfast. On the way home, my phone rang. It was Lisa.

"Have you been listening to the news?" she asked me. "A plane flew into one of the Twin Towers in New York. It looks really bad. Oh no, another one just flew into the other tower. Oh my God."

When I walked through the front door, I saw Lisa's packed suitcase sitting in the foyer.

Before I could ask her if she was still planning on going, a third plane crashed into the Pentagon. Lisa was a clinical nurse specialist on the burn unit at her hospital at that time. She immediately called work, knowing any survivors would be taken to her hospital.

The phones were jammed for an hour. When Lisa finally got through, her supervisor told her she didn't need to come in.

"That's great," I said, having no idea what it meant.

"No, it's not great. It's terrible," she told me. "It means there are barely any survivors. They're all gone. It's terrible."

Clear on what I wanted, I finally asked, "Are you still planning on going to LA?"

"I don't see how I can. I don't know how I'll tell Sandy," she explained. "If I go, I feel like I may never see you again, Paul. Leaving you doesn't feel right. I'm not going." Tears fell from her eyes.

I hugged her. I was relieved because I wasn't sure what I might have done or said to keep her from leaving. All I knew in that moment was that I couldn't imagine my life without Lisa in it.

Later that afternoon, we sat outside at the Evening Star Café in Del Ray, about three miles from Lisa's condo. The sky was crystal clear and the sun was brilliant. It could have been any other crisp fall afternoon, but that September day the air was filled with the sound of sirens and the smell of smoke from the Pentagon burning. When our food arrived, we barely touched it.

There were no planes departing from Dulles Airport that night. All commercial air traffic had been grounded by the FAA. Lying in bed on September 11, 2001, the only aviation noise we heard were F-16s patrolling overhead.

After turning off the light, Lisa rolled over and kissed me goodnight.

"You know the plane that crashed into the Pentagon was American Airlines flight 77? I would've been on that flight, but you wanted to spend more time with me. Did you know that?" she asked me.

"Yes," I said quietly. "I know."

I kissed her goodnight and for the first time I told her, "I love you."

She smiled at me, kissed my lips softly and whispered, "I know."

Chapter 5

Trusting Your Gut

Those memories and others drifted through my head as I dozed in my chair. We hadn't had Wrigley long, but I missed going to bed without carrying out our nightly ritual of walking around the lake together.

"What are you thinking about Paul?" Lisa asked, breaking my drifting consciousness. The experience at the animal hospital had wiped me out. When my mom was sick I had wanted to sleep all day. It was depressing sitting in her hospital room watching her die. Ironically, the experience felt like it was sucking the life out of me. When I saw Wrigley in that cage at the animal hospital, it brought back that same sense of helplessness I experienced with my mother's illness.

"Paul, are you ok?" Lisa asked.

"Yeah," I said, reaching a full attention span. "I was just thinking about everything. I was replaying what they told us about Wrigley being so sick. It happened so fast. It's scary. I'm not sure why I'm always surprised when I'm reminded how little we really control in life, or death, for that matter."

"That's so true," Lisa said. "I'm exhausted. You look like you are too. You ready to go up?"

I was about to say, "I'll be up after I walk Wrigley," but I stopped myself. I followed her to our bedroom.

I had no memory of Lisa getting up or leaving for work the next morning. I woke up at eight-thirty. It was the first morning in a long time that I didn't have to get up early to walk Wrigley. The extra sleep meant little to me.

I called the animal hospital before pouring my first cup of coffee. I wanted an update. They told me Wrigley's vet was on her morning rounds and would get back to me by ten.

I called back at ten-fifteen, but the vet was still unavailable. I decided to go over to the hospital and speak with someone face to face.

Wrigley was being treated at a veterinary teaching hospital. When I arrived, I was told that the vets and residents completed rounds together, thus no one was available to speak with me.

Margaret, a young lady wearing blue scrubs with colorful animals printed on them, met with me in place of a vet. She walked in with an attitude, not a smile. I sensed she found my request for an update on my sick puppy's condition unreasonable. Evidently, I was breaking protocol by showing up unannounced and demanding information about Wrigley. I knew immediately I didn't like her.

"Mr. Sullivan, Wrigley is a very sick dog," she said.

"No, shit. This is an emergency animal hospital, not a doggy day spa."

That's what I wanted to say, but I didn't. I listened to her tell me what I already knew.

"When Wrigley arrived yesterday morning his temperature was close to 105 degrees, and he was dehydrated. Last night his fever returned. His condition remains critical. He's not eating or sleeping. He's very sick," she repeated.

"I'm the one who carried him in here. I know how bad he was. Do you know why he's not getting better? What did the lab results say?" I asked.

"The vet will have to review those findings with you. I don't do that. I do know they're waiting to make a final diagnosis after the radiologist reads the x-rays," she told me.

"Nobody mentioned any x-rays to me, or my wife. We were supposed to be advised of any additional tests or costs. What did they x-ray?" I asked. My frustration peaked and I didn't give her an opportunity to answer. "You know, I don't like getting little bits and pieces of information. I want to speak with the vet, now."

"That's not possible," she responded.

"Three hours. That's how long it's been since I first called this morning. I'd like to at least see Wrigley while I'm here, waiting. And not back there, where he's stuck in that cage. I want to be with him here, where it's quiet," I told her.

"Moving Wrigley isn't a good idea. He's too weak and agitated. I can't recommend it."

I was thoroughly pissed off. It was ridiculous that a vet couldn't take five minutes from their rounds to talk with me. Margaret, in her animal pajama scrubs and high and mighty attitude, wasn't helping build my trust regarding Wrigley's care. I'd been diplomatic up until then, but I have limited tolerance for incompetence.

"I didn't ask for your recommendation, Margaret," I said. "But if it makes you feel better, I've taken what you've said into consideration. Now if you won't bring me my puppy, I need to speak with someone who will."

Margaret left the room angry. A few minutes later she walked in, pushing the door open with her butt. When she turned, facing me, I saw Wrigley. She placed him on the cold stainless steel examining table in the middle of the room.

"He shouldn't be disturbed like this. I'll be back in five minutes," she said.

Wrigley raised his head when he saw me. His eyes were oozing. I couldn't remember if we had told them about his ointment. He tried standing. I stopped him, and when I picked him up he let out a painful whimper. I held him close to my body. He didn't have his pleasant puppy smell.

I kissed his head while wiping the discharge from his eyes.

I put my coat on the exam table before laying Wrigley down. An IV catheter was taped to his right front leg. I couldn't believe how bad he looked. It was like staring at a different dog.

I pet him from his head to his tail slowly, over and over. He exhaled deeply, closed his eyes and started his familiar puppy snoring. I wanted to cry with relief that he recognized me. That gave me a little hope. He wasn't completely gone, but I think he was dying. He had that smell, that look.

Before my mom died of pancreatic cancer, I'd sit by her bed in the ICU. She'd tried to extend her life by six months to a year by agreeing to a difficult surgery. They stopped the last chance, life prolonging procedure halfway through and closed her up. The cancer was everywhere.

Afterward, she lay in bed alive because of machines and tubes. I was always scared of seeing someone in that condition. Up until that point in my life I had done a superb job of avoiding visiting people in those situations.

My mom was unconscious from the drugs. I'd never know for sure if she had an awareness I was sitting there. Surprisingly, being there brought me comfort though. That was my goal in seeing Wrigley. I wanted him to feel how much I cared.

Margaret said he wasn't sleeping. I thought of the noise and light in the ICU. It wasn't a peaceful place to recover. Wrigley was stuck in that cage all alone, and was probably scared to death. In these few minutes he was asleep with me, making puppy noises.

I whispered into Wrigley's little floppy ear. "You're a proud Great Dane puppy, Wrigley. I love you. Wrigley, you're a proud Great Dane puppy."

He opened his eyes. I felt like he understood. We both flinched when the door opened without warning.

Our moment ended with Margaret picking Wrigley up and retreating from the room without uttering a word.

I was tired of waiting around, so I left the hospital.

On my way home my phone rang. It was Lisa.

"I thought you said you were going to call me? How's Wrigley doing? Has he gotten any better?" she asked in Lisa fashion.

"I was just about to call you. I just left the hospital. I never spoke with a vet. They were too busy," I said.

"Too busy? What does that mean?"

"Honestly, I have no idea. I did see Wrigley though. The girl who brought him in was a total bitch."

I wanted to vent my anger and frustration. I'm sure the girl wasn't all bad, but she became the target of my unhappiness. I started going off.

"Honey, I've got to go. Can we talk about her later? How's Wrigley? Does he look better? Was he excited to see you?"

"He looks terrible, really bad. I think he was glad to see me, but he fell asleep," I said.

"Okay, my pager has gone off twice in the last minute. I really have to go. Anything else?" Lisa asked.

"I don't have a good feeling leaving Wrigley at that hospital. It's not just about the girl today either. It's the whole runaround and no answers. They took x-rays without asking us too. It doesn't feel right.

Nobody's talking to anybody; not even to me. I can't tell who's actually taking care of Wrigley. I want to take him to another hospital. Are you okay with that?"

"Paul, I know you love Wrigley. I wasn't there today, but if that's what you think, I'm fine with whatever you want to do. Promise to call me? I love you. Hug Wrigley for me. I have to go," she said, and our call ended.

Chapter 6

Too Late for Talking

I walked through the cat door entrance of the animal hospital at twelve forty-five PM.

"May I help you sir?" the receptionist asked.

"Yes, I'm here to pick up my puppy, Wrigley Sullivan."

"I'm sorry. You came through the wrong door. I can help you over here." She moved over to another computer.

Unbelievable. I moved over three feet, crossing over the painted red line.

"I can help you now. What's the dog's name again?" she asked.

"Wrigley Sullivan. He's a puppy, a Great Dane."

The lady took hold of a microphone similar to one you might see in an old Burger King commercial. She spoke into it, "Pick up in the front. Mr. Sullivan's waiting for Wrigley."

Someone came from behind the 'staff only' doors and conferred with the receptionist for a minute before she called me back up to the front desk. "Mr. Sullivan, nobody knows anything about Wrigley's discharge. Did you speak with someone earlier about it?"

"No, but a friend of mine gave me the name of another animal hospital where the vets actually talk with pet owners. I'm taking Wrigley there," I said.

I was quickly ushered into a private meeting room and speaking with a vet within three minutes. He tried to change my mind. In fairness, he agreed to take the charges off for the x-rays and was apologetic for the lack of communication. My mind was made up.

He gave me copies of the x-rays and promised to fax their findings and test results to the other hospital. I paid the $1076.00 bill without receiving any definitive diagnosis.

With Wrigley secure in my arms, I purposely crossed over the red line and walked out the cat door exit.

I paged Lisa. She called back in five minutes.

"I can't talk long. What's happening with Wrigley?"

"I have him with me," I said. "I'm taking him to the place that saved Bogie."

"Who? Where?" she asked.

Our friends Mark and Susan owned an English Bulldog. Two years ago, when their dog tore a tendon, it had required surgery. After the procedure their dog went into cardiac arrest while in recovery. Unfortunately, we had more in common with Mark and his wife than just an ailing dog. They had suffered three miscarriages in six years. Bogie's near-death experience occurred close to the anniversary of their last failed pregnancy. Mark's wife had been in her second term at five and a half months when they lost that baby. They had already decorated the nursery.

When Mark told me the dog was on life support, being kept alive by a respirator, I thought he was joking. He wasn't. The vet asked for permission to put their dog down, but Bogie had become their pseudo-child. The dog was their symbol of hope; a bright spot that represented a part of their healing.

My friend told the vet, "If you can save him, I want you to do it. I don't care how much it costs."

A canine cardiologist flew in from Denver the next day. I had no idea such a specialist even existed. The surgeon performed life saving surgery for Bogie. The total cost: $28,000. Fortunately my friend had enough money to afford it.

When he told me about saving Bogie I couldn't imagine spending that kind of money on a dog. At the time I had little understanding of what was behind his desperate attempt to save their pet.

With Wrigley's illness, I suddenly found myself with a much better recognition of what my friend had been going through. My empathy grew, frankly, from an experience I could have happily done without.

My graduate degree was in clinical social work, but I'd never committed to entering the field full-time. I facilitated a bereavement group at a hospice after graduating. Eventually I became a certified grief counselor and worked as a part-time volunteer at a local hospice for fifteen years.

It was common for people in the groups I led to explore whether it was easier to lose someone quickly and unexpectedly, in contrast to losing a loved one slowly from a long illness, allowing for an opportunity to say goodbye.

There is no right answer. Our loss from not being able to get pregnant couldn't compare to our friends' miscarriages. Was it really less devastating?

It didn't matter. The pain we all experienced was real. The scenario of how we reached a sad outcome didn't change or diminish the heartbreak.

All my training and experience aside, Wrigley was introducing me to a new twist in understanding how my friends had coped.

"Oh, Mark and Bogie," Lisa recalled. "Call me when you find out anything."

Wrigley was curled up, covered with a down comforter, lying on his magical driving sofa. I climbed in the back of the SUV after parking in the lot at the second animal hospital. I wanted a few minutes alone with him without any commotion around us. I put my head against his body, placed my hand on his head and whispered into his ear.

"I love you, Wrigley. I want you to get better, boy. You're a proud Great Dane puppy, Wrigley. Let's get you home. You need to get better, fella."

I believed my love and positive energy would help him. His eyes raised each time I said his name. I kissed his head, and he let out a sigh and slowly exhaled. I held him quietly for another minute, and then I gently carried him inside.

When I walked into the small lobby, everyone turned and watched as I carried our puppy towards the receptionist.

"He's adorable. Look at those paws. I know a puppy that's going to be spoiled here," the perky receptionist said, forcing a smile. Other staff members extended me a warm welcome and compliments for Wrigley. A playful argument about whether Wrigley was the cutest puppy they'd ever seen ensued.

Sadly, Wrigley showed little enthusiasm over the attention. He was sick.

After they took him back, I sat down and filled out the paperwork. What was I supposed to put under "medical history"? He was barely five months old.

I did my best and then handed the forms back to the receptionist.

It was just after three o'clock. I had not eaten breakfast or lunch, and I was starving.

"Would it be okay if I slipped out for a quick bite to eat? I'm just going across the street. You've got my cell if you need me." I pulled on my coat.

"That's fine. Don't worry about your little cutie. We'll take good care of him," she promised. I wanted to believe her, but something made me distrustful of her words. Her happy facade was a bit too perfect; maybe just a tad too rehearsed for me to feel it was completely sincere.

I went through the Arby's drive-thru because I didn't want to be around people. The sun was already beginning to set. I hated the short days after the time change. The angle of the sun warmed the inside of my SUV, acting like a drug. I dosed off after eating my roast beef sandwich and curly fries, remembering better times.

During high school my buddies and I would end our Friday and Saturday nights at the Roy Rogers restaurant that was walking distance from our neighborhood. We'd pile four inches of onions on our burgers, hoping to hide our beer breath from our parents.

My reminiscing ended abruptly when the door of the car next to mine slammed shut. It pulled me out of my easy semi-sleep state. I only napped for ten minutes, but I felt energized.

I'd only been away from the vet's office for twenty-five minutes. I wasn't in a big rush to get back and sit in their waiting room. When my mom was dying, I'd leave the hospital for lunch each day around noon, walk to the same local deli and eat alone at a table while listening to people's conversations. It was bizarre to sit next to my dying mother one minute, then be engulfed minutes later in the minutia of everyday life. Hearing someone bitching about too much mayonnaise on their sandwich left me feeling very disconnected from the rest of the world, but it was a reminder that the earth was still spinning outside her hospital room.

Important things that really mattered were clear to me then. I wish I could hold onto that perspective more often. Gaining that knowledge came with a heavy price, however.

I remember one nurse who'd refused to give my mother additional pain medication, saying my mom had declined it. My mom was in no condition to make decisions or give rational answers. She declined the medication for fear of becoming addicted. She would be dead within a week. Addiction was the last concern we had for her. The nurse was removed from my mother's care. The entire idea of my mom being denied any relief infuriated me and still does.

I wondered if my feeling of powerlessness over my mother's pancreatic cancer was the reason I had moved Wrigley to this animal hospital. Moving him made me feel empowered. I was sure the first place wasn't providing what Wrigley needed to get better. I was pleased with myself for trusting my instincts, especially since I wasn't normally this decisive or bold.

I didn't want to lose Wrigley. I wanted to do the best I could for him.

I finally went back inside to wait and very soon after met with the vet, Dr. Harmon. He was a handsome man in his forties with a full head of hair. My hair was thinning in the back. Hairline envy was new for me, and as I caught myself thinking about it, I knew I needed a Ritalin but, once again, I didn't have any with me.

I did my best to sit quietly and listen as the vet went over Wrigley's condition.

"Wrigley's resting comfortably. His fever has been stabilized. A very good sign too is that he ate half a cup of kibble. His left rear leg is our primary focus of concern. We received the lab work and reviewed the x-rays from the other hospital. We'd like to take another set of pictures," he said.

He raised his head after reading from the chart to see if I had any questions. I didn't. He continued.

"Dr. Bonnet is our large dog specialist. She's in surgery now, but I'd like her to examine Wrigley and get her insight on what's happening. She's an expert in bone disease. A bone marrow sample would identify or rule out stenosis," he said.

I'd lost my concentration. I didn't know what stenosis was and lacked the focus to ask. My ADD was operating at full power.

"Mr. Sullivan? Anything else I can explain?" he asked.

In grammar school, my pencil often rolled off my desk onto the floor when I fell asleep during class. When the vet asked me if I had any "further questions" it reminded me of when my teachers caught me sleeping.

"The lameness in his left leg," I said, pretending I hadn't been zoning out. "That's the area where Wrigley had his vaccine shot Saturday. Everything happened after that. Is it possible there is a connection?"

I was convinced Wrigley's current condition and the shot were related, but Dr. Harmon shared the same conclusion with the previous hospital. It was a coincidence, not the cause.

After our meeting ended I returned to the waiting area to obtain the cost of Wrigley's treatment. It would only be an estimate. While I was waiting for the numbers to be crunched, I remembered that Dr. Shiller's office was open. I'd never make it to his clinic by five with rush hour already starting, but I wanted to speak with him. I wanted his opinion. I trusted him.

I stepped outside the hospital and called Dr. Shiller's clinic.

JoAnn, Dr. Shiller's assistant, loved Wrigley and felt terrible when I told her what had happened. She interrupted Dr. Shiller in the middle of an exam so he could talk with me.

I appreciated the gesture very much.

I described everything that had occurred with Wrigley in the last day and a half. Finally, I heard what I believed to be a voice of reason.

"It seems to me Wrigley had a severe reaction to the vaccine," Dr. Shiller told me. "It does happen. You just hope it never happens to your pet. I'm sorry for everything you're going through," he said.

I knew Dr. Shiller would be straightforward with me. I asked him the most important question on my mind.

"If I take Wrigley home, out of this hospital, do you think he'd make it through the night? Based on what I've told you, do you think he's dying?"

"I'm sure the worst of it is over. Plan on bringing Wrigley in tomorrow morning first thing, say eight o'clock. Follow the course the hospital gave you with his medications. His temperature needs to be watched closely, though. If it passes 104 he needs to go back to the hospital. Otherwise he should be fine overnight. We'll sort this out tomorrow. We'll get a plan to get your boy back on his feet." He reconfirmed the eight o'clock time again before hanging up.

The last trace of the sun was sinking behind the tree line over the west end of the parking lot. It was cold. I went back inside.

The receptionist held out some papers for me. "I thought maybe you went out for another snack," she said with her forced smile. "Dr. Harmon itemized each treatment option for your convenience.

Whichever plan you decide upon, you'll need to pay in full before leaving. Let me know if you have any questions."

Once again, I could tell she'd repeated that to customers a thousand times.

I desperately needed a Ritalin. I imagined her nose as a "delete" or "disappear" button. I wanted to push it firmly with my index finger. I swear everyone sitting in the waiting area was staring at me as I walked back to my seat.

At least three people glanced away hurriedly when I looked up. Lisa says I get paranoid sometimes, but this was real. I wasn't imagining it.

"Feels like I should hear a drum roll or something," I said to the guy sitting across from me.

He started leafing through an old copy of Time magazine instead of responding to me, which I found rude. "The Person of the Year" on the cover staring at me was the choice from two years earlier, unless that same person had won again. Anything is possible.

I flipped to the last page of Dr. Harmon's recommended treatment plan for Wrigley. The bottom line read, "Estimated cost: $2545.00-$3600.00. Minimum payment due immediately: $2545.00."

I was glad Dr. Shiller had talked to me. Lisa's hospital had to be extremely busy because she'd been unable to respond to the page I'd sent her during lunch.

I returned to the receptionist.

"How did you want to pay?" she asked. "Checks are fine. If you use a credit card, we don't accept American Express. I hope that's not a problem."

I'm guessing my hesitation over answering her assumptive questions led her to believe I was in need of financial help.

"We do pet payment agreements and also accept pet insurance should anything happen in the future. Let me get you a brochure. So you know, we're not affiliated with this group, but I can process the application here, right now. Does that help you?" she asked.

"That's okay, thanks." I pulled out my wallet. "I want to pay for just the services you've already provided. I'm going to take Wrigley home now. Would you please let them know I'm waiting for Wrigley?"

I had the undivided attention of the staff and all those sitting in the waiting area.

The receptionist's perky, glued-on smile disappeared. "I'm not sure exactly how to do this. I'll have to speak with Dr. Harmon. I'm sure he'll want to speak with you before discharging Wrigley. Are you sure you don't want a brochure?" she asked me again as if it was the first time.

"I'm sure," I said, returning to my seat.

The guy across from me set down his Time magazine. "Now that deserved a drum roll."

I was sitting across from Dr. Harmon within five minutes. He was concerned about my decision.

"It's certainly your right to take Wrigley home. It is, however, my responsibility to educate you about the dangers he's facing and explain why his condition is serious. We want to help you find the cause of his illness and offer you the best way to treat it. It's important Wrigley stay overnight. His fever is erratic and could return. He's also on an IV drip. Maybe I can help you select the most economical treatment plan for him," he said.

My ADD was in full gear. My mind was racing all over. I pictured the veterinarian hosting a new kind of "Let's Make a Deal" reality show. On this show, contestants picked what was behind door number 1, door number 2, or door number 3 in hopes of finding the best treatment plan to save their puppy.

I wanted to flip the channel.

The vet was doing his job. I didn't doubt he was concerned about Wrigley. The money issue was important, but it was secondary. I truly believed Wrigley wasn't going to get better unless he came home. Lisa and I needed to remind him of why he wanted to survive.

"With all due respect, I'd like to take Wrigley home. My wife's a nurse; she can handle the IV. I'm tired. It's not my intention to engage in a negotiation over Wrigley's treatment. I know you have costs. I appreciate what you provided him today. I'm ready to take him home," I said.

The vet knew our discussion was closed.

An attendant unceremoniously handed Wrigley over to me. Our puppy didn't look much better than when we had arrived, but he perked up when he saw me. It helped reassure me that I was making the best decision for him and me.

I had been hoping for a sign that I was doing the right thing, and his reaction was enough for me. I wasn't clear if the receptionist, the staff behind her desk or the folks in the waiting area saw me walk out with Wrigley in my arms or if they intentionally ignored us. No one held the door open for me or said goodbye to arguably, "the cutest puppy they'd ever seen."

The cold November air felt good against my face. I was glad to be out of animal hospitals. I noticed how clear the sky was when I set Wrigley down in the SUV and covered him up with his comforter.

He rolled his head in half circles, swaying back and forth. I think he was happy to be back lying down on his magic sofa with wheels. Maybe he was aware he was on his way home. That's what I wanted to believe.

I leaned over and kissed his nose and massaged behind his ears with both my hands.

"Sorry for all the crap you just went through, buddy. You know I love you, Wrigley. I'm never leaving you like that again, ever. Now who's my proud Great Dane puppy? You, Wrigley. You are. You're my proud Great Dane puppy. Wrigley Sullivan, you handsome boy."

He closed his eyes and signed off with a long sigh. He slept comfortably the entire way as I navigated us home at the peak of rush hour. The traffic didn't bother me a bit.

Once we got home, I set Wrigley down on the grass.

He peed for a long time. When I moved to pick him up, he was already moving toward the breezeway, his left rear leg dragging behind. It was out of sequence with his other legs but he pushed forward.

I wanted to pick him up, but he kept moving, determined to make it on his own.

I grabbed him once he reached the door. Tears blurred my vision. I felt like I was watching one of those inspirational endings to the Ironman competition where a handicapped athlete pulls his body over the finish line in triumph.

"Welcome home, Wrigley! You really are a proud Great Dane puppy," I said as I carried him into the house.

That night Lisa and I didn't sleep well, but Wrigley slept like a baby. The "no dog in bed" rule was suspended once again.

"He's convalescing," Lisa explained. "I see it at the hospital all the time. When someone is loved and has friends and family surrounding them, their recovery goes much smoother. I feel bad for people alone in hospitals. It's sad."

I know she was trying to guarantee Wrigley could continue to sleep in our bed.

I also knew that if a patient were dying on Lisa's watch and had no one with them, Lisa would sit and hold their hand until they passed.

"No one should die alone unless they want to, Paul. I'd want to know someone cared if I was alone and dying." She had shared that thought with me after my mom died. She was trying to help me heal by pointing out that my mom was surrounded by her kids and love when she passed. What she shared helped me at a time when I wasn't sure anyone could.

Tuesday morning Lisa and I were convinced Wrigley was not ready or willing to die. He ate some food and drank a bowl of water before his appointment with Dr. Shiller. His temperature was normal. The antibiotics and anti-inflammatory medication were working. His left rear leg remained a big problem, but he was in much better spirits.

Lisa and I waited in the parking lot that morning and watched as Dr. Shiller pulled in. He waved for us to come in even though it wasn't yet eight o'clock.

"He's past the worst part of the reaction," Dr. Shiller said after examining him. "He's got a ways to go in building up that leg muscle. That's going to be critical if he's going to walk normally again. He needs his strength to exercise. That's the key," he instructed.

Within two weeks, Wrigley had learned to use his hurt leg as a crutch, balancing himself by bouncing off that leg every other step while he walked. His appetite returned.

Dr. Shiller had said we'd know within a month if he would fully recuperate. Lisa and I read all kinds of literature about vaccine reactions and the best methods to help a dog recover. We concluded there was a lot of conflicting information on how to proceed with Wrigley's recovery. It was confusing and frustrating. There didn't appear to be any concrete, simple or easy answers. It was a situation we'd find ourselves in again, in the not so distant future.

Chapter 7

The Recovery

I bought a dog life preserver for Wrigley. Lisa was convinced I had lost my mind. I reaffirmed her belief when I climbed into the hot tub off the lower deck with Wrigley and massaged his left rear leg while he sat on my lap.

At first the bubbles and steam scared the hell out of him, and he tried jumping out of my arms. But there was no place for him to escape.

By our third aqua therapy session I think Wrigley looked forward to our spa time together. One afternoon, I found Lisa in the hot tub with Wrigley.

"He jumped in," she said with a coy smile.

"Really," I said. "He put that life jacket on all by himself?"

We decided a raw diet for Wrigley might help him recover faster. Dr. Shiller wasn't a proponent of the idea. He told us he knew too many people getting sick from salmonella after handling raw poultry. Dr. Shiller's warning didn't deter us from going to Costco and purchasing large packs of beef and chicken. We'd measure it out, cut it up and put it in Ziploc bags. It was a pain to do and expensive, but Wrigley ate and loved it.

He was a huge fan of raw liver and chicken hearts too. He ate them like popcorn. His favorite treat was chewing on pig ears. He could easily eat a bag of those in a week.

Wrigley quickly regained the eight pounds he'd lost after the shot and added another fourteen pounds within five weeks. He was growing fast, but his left rear leg wasn't keeping up. The muscle on that upper quadrant was larger, but the rest of his leg was thin and weak. His paw on that leg was notably smaller than the others as well.

We resumed short walks around the lake despite the cold temperatures and occasional snow flurries. Wrigley was warm in his winter fleece and an overcoat that I bought for him. Despite his enthusiasm for the walks, we never made it past the bench that was halfway along the dam wall because Wrigley grew tired or it became obvious his leg hurt. Not wanting him to get worse, I never pushed him past his limits. We'd simply turn around and head for home.

Wrigley's dog friends in the neighborhood stopped visiting after his illness. Lisa and I could tell people felt uncomfortable seeing him. He wasn't capable of playing fetch or roughhousing anymore. I imagine it was sad for people having seen him before and watching him now.

I was just happy he was alive and back at home with us. I felt confident Wrigley would get better and the worst was behind us.

A month passed. Wrigley weighed 44 pounds. His Great Dane features became more distinctive. His snout was full and his jowls were forming. His chest was becoming much wider, stockier.

People didn't ask what kind of dog he was anymore; it was obvious. It was also obvious there was something wrong with his back leg, because it slid out from under his body if he stood in one place too long. Some people asked point blank while others stared, looked away or simply ignored him. His constant repositioning of his leg made other dogs nervous. The welcoming energy Wrigley had come to expect from his fellow canines was unfortunately replaced with defensive and sometimes aggressive energy from other dogs. I could tell Wrigley was confused by the messages coming from his canine colleagues. He wanted to play, but they wouldn't engage with him anymore. Before he got sick, Wrigley's favorite game was tug-of-war. I continued playing it with him on the sofa as he slowly adjusted to his weakened leg.

After six weeks, Wrigley was fairly stable on three legs. He'd push his right leg out and balance off the bad one when he started losing his footing.

One day I walked up the hill on the side of the house, and I kicked an old ball he used to play with before getting sick. He ran to it. It wasn't a normal run, it was more of a hop. It was the first time I'd seen him move like that since he'd been sick.

I ran to the top of the hill to see if he'd follow me. When I turned around I didn't see him because he was standing alongside of me. He'd kept up with me by hopping along.

"I knew you could do it, Wrigley! You're amazing, buddy. Wait 'til Lisa hears about this." I gave him a huge hug.

Wrigley's tail whipped against my leg. I think he was proud and excited about his accomplishment.

The cats knew that something was different with Wrigley, and they had made adjustments too. Zoe had started following us on our short walks, but stayed a safe distance away from Wrigley and the water.

Cassie had become his snuggle-buddy while he was recovering. She'd curled up next to him on the sofa when he was unable to get up or down by himself. I saw Wrigley lick her little face once. She ran away, but the gesture was a testament to their trust and solid friendship. They forged a sweet bond during that period.

Precious remained aloof as the only other four-legged male in the house.

Two weeks before Christmas as Lisa and I walked Wrigley in the backyard along the lake, I asked her, "Do you think Wrigley will ever be completely healthy? Not healthy, but normal? You know what I mean."

"Wrigley's going to be a special needs dog, Paul. He's always going to exhibit signs of a handicap. He doesn't know anything's wrong with him though. Look at him. He pushes ahead the best he can. He's a loved dog. Even with his problems, he's a happy puppy," she reassured me.

Lisa stopped then, and looked at me. "Paul, I need to talk to you about something."

Whenever she used that tone and those words my gut would tighten. I'm not sure when that reflex began in our relationship, but I prepared for a serious talk, one that often involved something I was doing that was not appreciated.

"Yeah. Okay. What is it?" I felt like I had just stepped on glass with bare feet.

"It's not about you, Paul. Relax," she said, taking my hand.

"It's been almost two months since all this started. Dr. Shiller said it was fine letting Wrigley do whatever he wants if it helps build his leg muscle. I was thinking, and please let me finish without interrupting me, that maybe if Wrigley had a dog companion, he'd do better." She then stopped talking and remained silent, waiting for my objections. This was a classic Lisa sell job. She'd have an answer ready for any of my objections. She was always very organized in her rebuttal and justifications for why I was wrong.

"Why don't you think we can exercise him? Another dog is an added responsibility that I'll be stuck with while you're at work," I said. "You don't think I'm doing a good job with his rehab?"

"Honey, it's not that at all. You've been amazing with Wrigley. It's why he's doing as well as he is. But you're not a dog. I saw you yesterday with him on the side of the house. It was so pathetic and cute at the same time. I couldn't believe you had that disgusting rope in your mouth, down on your hands and knees, playing tug-of-war with him.

"I live here too, you know. People are going to think you've lost it. But to answer you directly, you've done a phenomenal job with Wrigley. I think another dog would make it easier on you, actually. Wrigley relies on you for everything.

"When was the last time you went out with your friends? Plus, you know Wrigley's a dog's dog. He's happiest playing with other dogs. I get sad knowing he's missing that in his life since he got hurt." Lisa began to tear up.

I hugged her, and Wrigley pushed between our legs. We both looked down while he looked up at us. "I think he understands more than we give him credit for," I said.

"You're probably right, Lisa. I've become preoccupied with him. Maybe another dog would help him and free up my time. Reality is I'll never be a legitimate dog substitute. What kind of dog is the big question? I'm not up for another Great Dane."

Lisa agreed. Finding Wrigley a companion would be tricky. He was so clumsy and still growing. He might hurt a little dog by accident. But a big dog might hurt Wrigley while they played.

We decided to start looking for another pup after the holidays passed, beyond New Years. It was a good plan that wouldn't hold long.

We were finding out early with Wrigley that our plans often met with an unexpected fork in the road.

Three days later Don, Wrigley's breeder, called Lisa. He'd stayed in contact with us after finding out what had happened with Wrigley. He'd been sympathetic and even offered to take Wrigley back, which was never a consideration for us. We knew he'd probably have put Wrigley down.

After ending the call, Lisa came into the living room looking unsettled.

"What's going on?" I asked.

Wrigley raised his head off the arm of the sofa and stared at Lisa. "That was Don. He called to ask us for a favor."

"Really. After everything with Wrigley, he wants a favor? He's got some balls, doesn't he?" I said dismissively.

"What happened with Wrigley wasn't Don's fault, Paul. Wrigley just has problems. Anyway, he called to tell us he's been assigned to Kuwait for a year. His daughter's getting married next month and moving to California. He said he doesn't have anybody to manage his farm," she said. I interrupted her.

"Lisa. Please just tell me what favor Don wants from us. Don't get me wrong. I'm very happy for his daughter. I wish her the best, but I really don't care." I was more interested in getting back to the TV show I was watching.

"He wants to know if we want to adopt Wrigley's half-sister. It's his daughter's puppy, but she can't take the dog with her to California. They thought of us because of everything we've been through with Wrigley."

Lisa rubbed her arms. "It's freaky. We just talked about getting another dog three days ago. I've got chills."

I had to admit, the timing was bizarre. The one breed we'd absolutely ruled out was practically being gift wrapped and delivered to our door. Only because it was Wrigley's half-sister did we consider it, but knowing the cost of a purebred Great Dane made Don's offer even more attractive. The circumstances were almost too serendipitous to believe.

Lisa felt the same way, and she was beside herself with excitement. She was so cute when she was energized with enthusiasm. Her eyes sparkled with life when she was exuberant. She was reminding me of our first date, when she discovered I had a good sense of humor and started laughing at my jokes. We were only starting to know one another. I immediately recognized a childlike playfulness with Lisa that I loved about her. When she shared that side of herself with me, my mind and heart were in one place only, with her in that moment. It was different now from when we'd first met. It wasn't more or better, but it was different. We knew each other on a deeper level because of our shared experiences; good and bad. Lisa didn't carry around unresolved baggage and it showed. Her smile lit up a room, putting people at ease. I loved making her laugh and she was a great audience. Even during times that pushed us to the brink we found a way to laugh. It probably saved our relationship. It was something that happened naturally for us. It never felt forced. Wrigley helped bring that back into our lives. He was a blessing, if for only that reason alone.

Even when I was mad or unhappy with Lisa I never stopped liking her. I think that sustained me more than love during our difficult periods. My love for her obliged me to work things out, but enjoying our friendship and liking Lisa was my motivation for staying and holding onto hope for our future together.

The idea of having two Great Danes piqued our imaginations.

"Let's do it, Lisa. I think it'll be awesome. Two of them, crazy," I said, shaking my head in disbelief at how quickly we backtracked on our original plan.

Lisa started jumping up and down, swinging her hands in the air, before rushing over to Wrigley. "Are you ready for some Great Dane girl-power, Wrigley?" She shot up and jumped on me, almost pushing me over. "I'm so excited. I'm so happy you want her too! She may be Wrigley's half-sister, but she's going to bring us twice the fun!"

Chapter 8

Best Christmas Ever

The puppy was a beautiful slender black Great Dane. Her pictures showed an oddly shaped patch of white fur on her chest, white frosted paws and a dab of white fur surrounding her snout. Her tail was nearly identical to Wrigley's, looking as though it had been dipped in a bucket of white paint. Her markings were faint and washed out compared to Wrigley's strongly contrasting white and black coat.

"She's pretty," Lisa said, touching the computer screen with her finger.

I don't mean to equate having met my wife to meeting this dog, but it happened in a similar fashion. Bob, a good friend of mine, and I had shared a group house with ten guys and ten girls in Dewey Beach, Delaware, for several years during our single lives after graduate school.

One summer at the beach I introduced Bob to a young lady named Tracy. He was immediately smitten. She barely had time to walk away before he asked me, "Can you get me her number?"

They were married a year and a half later. Bob was my last single friend to tie the knot, leaving me the lone bachelor. Twenty-six of Bob's closest friends and I headed to Las Vegas for his bachelor party. Before the airport limo arrived at the house, Tracy, now Bob's fiancé, showed me a picture of six women, all tanned, smiling and dressed in bright summer clothes posing in front of their beach house for their annual group photo. I knew several of the ladies in the picture.

Tracy mentioned that one of the girls had broken up with a guy, a doctor, that she'd been dating for five years. Six months had passed from that breakup, which was the exact time I'd been apart from my last girlfriend.

"I think you guys would hit it off," Tracy told me. "She's quiet at first, but really sweet and a lot of fun. She loves to laugh, so you should get along." Tracy handed me the picture. "Pick out the one girl you'd like to go out with, Paul."

My eyes immediately found the tallest girl in the middle of the group. Her smile was beautiful and enhanced by her brilliant white teeth. Her eyes sparkled with energy. Her skin was tan, a golden bronze. I loved how her long blonde hair naturally fell over her shoulders. I could tell by her body she was athletic. Her arms and legs were toned and fit. It sounds like the stuff in sappy movies and bad romance novels, but I knew at that moment I was going to marry her. She was beautiful, and I wanted her in my life.

Of all my friends who had married, half were divorced or wished they were. Some had even cheated while they were engaged, never honestly giving their relationship a chance.

I'd never considered getting married until I saw Lisa's picture and something "clicked" inside of me. Maybe it was simply timing, but when I saw her I knew she was the one for me.

Supposedly, people have their desired mate's profile etched in their subconscious by the age of five. My first crush was on Tammy Hinkle when I was in the first grade. I wrote down her name on the inside pocket of my school folder. When it fell open on the school bus, leaving her name exposed for everyone to see, the whole bus chanted, "Paul and Tammy, sitting in a tree…"

I wasn't embarrassed, but relieved she finally knew who held my heart. Of course she was in third grade, a friend of my sister, and after the revelation Tammy never visited our home again.

Lisa was a mature, sexy version of my Tammy Hinkle. Physically, Lisa was incredibly attractive, but realistically, I didn't know her. But I wanted to find out if she was as sweet as her photo indicated.

When I returned home from Vegas, I called the number Tracy gave me, but only reached Lisa's answering machine. I left a message.

I called again a week later, leaving another message.

Two weeks passed without her calling me back.

I tried once more, a third time, and left her my final message, "I'm guessing you have a lot on your plate right now, so I won't call again. If I did, you might have me arrested for stalking. Sorry we didn't connect. Tracy said we'd hit it off. I was looking forward to meeting you. Maybe in another life. Take care."

Lisa called me back that night, and we talked for over two hours. Her mom was visiting, and had heard all three of the messages I'd left Lisa. She told Lisa after we'd finally connected on the phone, "I don't know why honey, but I swear you're going to marry that man."

Lisa's response was, "That's crazy, Mom. You can't tell anything over the phone. Anyway, he sounds chubby."

"Now *that's* crazy," her mom replied.

Lisa later told me she was relieved after opening her door on our initial date, which was a first "blind date" for both of us. My eyes are hazel, and I've been told my smile is warm. I carried my 220 pounds along a long torso, creating the illusion I was much trimmer than the scale indicated. The important thing was that Lisa found me attractive.

When she opened her door that night and saw me for the first time, standing at six feet and one inch with brown hair, an athletic body, and a smile with dimples, Lisa liked what she saw.

We went out to dinner and talked the entire time. Lisa wasn't accustomed to drinking vodka tonics, and in my enthusiasm to introduce them to her, she got a little tipsy. We were having such a good time, we closed down the Evening Star Cafe that Thursday night.

A blanket of snow had covered everything outside by the time we left. I pressed her body against my Jeep Cherokee and kissed her before opening her door.

"What do you think you're doing? Are you some kind of wise guy?" she asked me with a tentative smile.

"I wanted an early kiss goodnight. In case you jump out of the car once I get you home," I said, hoping that idea was not in her plans. Honestly, I hadn't been able to resist her. She was so adorable. I hoped she hadn't taken offense.

We drove back to her place, but she didn't invite me up. We talked in the lobby of her condo, near the mailboxes, for a half an hour.

"If you're not going to kiss me goodnight, I'll have to kiss you," she finally said, pushing me against the wall.

After her earlier hesitation, I had no clue what to make of the situation. We made out like high school kids for over twenty minutes.

"Let's go up," I said.

She pulled back. "I can't invite you up."

"Really? Why not?"

"Because I don't know you," she replied.

That was six years ago. She still confuses me at times.

But today there was no guessing about what Lisa or I were thinking.

We wanted that puppy.

Don had our answer in minutes, and we arranged to pick up Wrigley's half-sister the following night at the same place we had picked up Wrigley four months earlier.

When Don's white Ford pickup drove into the WaWa parking lot, I lifted Wrigley out of the back of our SUV and set him down on the parking lot pavement.

The dog in the crate sitting in the back of Don's truck was howling.

Wrigley rarely barked and had never howled.

As soon as Don opened the crate door, a stunning black Great Dane jumped out. Don held her collar, keeping her in place.

Wrigley's nose lifted high into the air. He was focused across the lot, and started pulling me forward with his leash.

"Easy, Wrigley." I was unfamiliar with him taking that kind of initiative.

Both the dogs pulled towards each other, meeting in the middle of the lot. Their noses touched briefly. Wrigley circled around the other puppy, his black nose disappearing under her tail. Five seconds later, his greeting was reciprocated by the other puppy. They jumped up, then dropped down low on their front paws, moving their bodies against each other, sharing a mutual excitement.

"There's a happy reunion," Don said. "They boarded together the last few weeks I had Wrigley. It looks like they remember each other."

Lisa thanked Don and asked him to relay our thanks to his daughter for offering her puppy to us. We were grateful.

After saying goodbye, Lisa returned to the spot she had first played with Wrigley, but this time there were two puppies alongside of her.

Don handed me Wrigley's half-sister's paperwork. I was relieved to find out she had already received her shots.

Don spoke slowly, almost like he was thinking out loud, when we shook hands goodbye.

"Wrigley's coming along. I didn't expect that from him." He looked over at the two puppies playing with Lisa. "He's filling out nicely.

Put those two together and you'd have a beautiful litter. You could make some good money too."

I was caught off guard by his departing statement. Surely he knew dogs so closely related should never be bred together. My gut churned thinking he might not know or worse, might not care. I walked slowly over to Lisa and the puppies. I never forgot his passing comment, and it heightened my awareness that breeding animals was ultimately a profit-making business.

Driving back home I acted as a chauffeur for two puppies and Lisa, because she chose to stay in the back of the Yukon and play with Wrigley and his new friend.

Once we were home, I opened the rear hatch. The new puppy jumped out with ease. I wasn't used to that.

Lisa climbed out afterwards while Wrigley waited for me to lift him out, whining and whimpering, anxious to join his new companion already on the front lawn.

"Should I let Zoe outside and put Precious and Cassie in the library?" Lisa asked. Her question reminded me of the introduction process we had completely ignored with Wrigley.

"They'll all be fine. Wrigley's already rocked their world. Zoe's not going to mess with a dog this big. My concern is more with how the new puppy reacts to the cats than how the cats react to her," I said.

As I had predicted, the cats showed limited interest in their new housemate. Cassie ran upstairs. Precious didn't move from his favorite cushion, and Zoe ran out the door when we walked in. Lisa didn't try to stop her.

Neither of us wanted to cook. We ordered a pizza and had a few beers. Instead of TV, we watched puppies.

"Let's name her tonight," Lisa suggested.

"She already has a name. It should be Riley because that was Wrigley's runner-up name, remember? Don't Wrigley and Riley sound good together?" I was hoping to avoid another naming crisis.

"Riley is a boy's name. The puppy is a girl," Lisa pointed out.

"Who cares about rules? They are dogs. She's not going to know. Other dogs won't know either. I'm voting Riley," I decided.

"I say...I love it, too," Lisa agreed with a laugh. "The gender thing was holding me back. But you're right, who cares? Wrigley and Riley Sullivan. I think they're meant to be together. Look at them. I think they love each other, just like us, sweetie." Lisa blew me a soft kiss. I pretended it pushed my face to one side.

I noticed some tomato sauce from the pizza on Lisa's chin, but I didn't bring it to her attention. I loved her, tomato sauce and all. Plus, I had learned that when your wife is being affectionate, pointing out the mundane is not really a smart play or appreciated.

"Wrigley is way past convalescing." I knew Lisa was going to bring this issue up sooner rather than later so I decided to beat her to it. "He's more than capable of getting on and off the sofa by himself. I think he could jump in the SUV too, but he likes me to lift him in and out for some reason. But I think it's time our big boy learns what it is like to share his own bed, or sofa, now."

Precious and Cassie didn't waste any time returning to our bed with Wrigley back downstairs. He didn't miss our bed, not even for a minute. Wrigley and Riley spooned on the sofa, like lovers, starting their first night together.

Lisa claimed she possessed powers allowing her to understand animal moods by the way their tails moved. She often identified when Precious was happy or angry by the smallest wave of his fluffy tail. There was no detectable difference from one tail flick to the other or within his mood as far as I could tell.

Lisa, apparently possessed the gift with the new puppy as well because she claimed Riley was kind and considerate with Wrigley because the puppy understood that Wrigley was special. She also believed Riley was grateful to us for rescuing her when her owner had to give her up.

"You can't see how appreciative she is? Look into her eyes. Watch how she wags her tail when you say her new name," Lisa instructed me. "You just don't have the gift, Paul," she explained.

Riley was a perfect athletic specimen in canine terms. She ran and jumped effortlessly. She was smart too. Lisa taught her to roll, sit and speak within a week. Wrigley could do all that too, but only when he wanted to, not on anybody's command.

Wrigley's neighborhood dog friends reappeared after we brought Riley into our home. Doggy playtime resumed on the side of our house. But playing tug-of-war with Wrigley perplexed most dogs. Because of his handicap, he learned to spin in a circle, protecting his vulnerable leg. It made it almost impossible for another dog to grab ahold of the rope while he spun.

If a dog became aggressive with Wrigley, Riley stepped in. She let other dogs know she intended to protect Wrigley from any threat.

At this point in time the puppies were just over six months old, but already as big or bigger than any of the other dogs in the neighborhood. Warning growls from either of our pups weren't easy to ignore.

* * *

We decorated our Christmas tree the weekend just after Riley joined our family. The puppies wanted to sniff every decoration before we hung it on the tree. When a blown glass ornament fell and broke on the floor, Wrigley ran and jumped for safety on his sofa.

Riley wasn't fazed by the noise. She stayed close to Lisa. I think she knew Wrigley and I had a special bond. She didn't show any desire to come between us or any sign of resentment because of it either. Riley was content becoming Lisa's girl, her special "sisterhood" puppy.

When I was a kid, five years old, my family celebrated a Christmas when I literally received every gift I asked Santa to bring me. I hadn't behaved especially well that year either. That only added to my excitement and surprise.

I watched as Lisa tried to put Santa hats on the puppies' heads for a picture in front of the tree. Wrigley shook his hat off each time I was about to snap a photo. Riley, on the other hand, obediently submitted to the indignity.

That year in our new home, with Lisa, the cats, Wrigley and Riley, I felt a sense of peace and joy I'd never experienced before. I'd always wondered if that childhood Christmas would ever be topped or even matched. But as I watched Lisa trying to put those silly hats on the dogs, I knew my memory of the best Christmas ever was being replaced with a new family memory.

Chapter 9

Have You Noticed

My aunt Marie moved in with my grandma after my grandfather died. My dad was only sixteen at the time. The sisters lived together the rest of their lives, over fifty years. It was always Grandma and Aunt Marie. Their names were never said apart while I was growing up. That's how it was with Wrigley and Riley. They ate together, played together and slept together.

Despite watching Riley effortlessly jump in and out of the SUV, Wrigley waited for me to lift him in and out. He was strong and growing, but there was little progress with his left leg. He'd mastered running, although he resembled a big bunny, hopping in unison off his back legs while pulling himself forward with his front. His chest and stocky upper body muscles were well developed.

Wrigley adjusted for what he lacked and maximized the use of what he had. Although Wrigley weighed more, eighty-five pounds in February, Riley's stature was more impressive because of her easy stance and ability to glide when in motion.

In late February, the DC metro area was hit by an unpredicted snow storm with its heaviest accumulations in the western suburbs of Northern Virginia, where we lived. The dogs went crazy running and sliding down the hill while fighting for the tug-of-war rope in the deep snow. The powder allowed Wrigley to push off his left rear leg, building his confidence. Riley never took advantage of Wrigley's handicap, but she intensified her play as he became bolder.

I never allowed other dogs to play as rough with Wrigley as Riley, because I trusted she wouldn't hurt him.

Another big snow storm followed in early March. Wrigley wore a fleece wrap and an overcoat that buckled under and around his chest and belly. Riley was fine without any additional cover. The dogs showed no signs of wanting to come inside, despite playing for over an hour in the wet snow. Lisa's southern blood froze in twenty minutes outside, leaving me to referee the winter dog games. I didn't mind at all. It was great watching the pups have so much fun. It made Lisa and me laugh out loud when we watched a video of their shenanigans later on.

After the early March snow melted daffodils could be seen pushing up from the ground. Those flowers were a tease. In Virginia, the daffodils blooming usually meant another decent snow storm would be coming, or at least a hard freeze. The lawn on the side of our house, the ground for many of Wrigley and Riley's epic tug-of-war battles, was decimated. It was nothing but mud that had been churned by large Great Dane dog paws.

I remember the day in mid-March when I watched Riley take the tug-of-war rope to Wrigley, trying to engage him in a match. Wrigley grabbed the rope, but stopped playing after a minute and forfeited the rope in front of Riley. I didn't make much of it, thinking only he'd become bored playing the game over a long winter.

Two weeks before my birthday. Lisa asked me, "Do you want to take the dogs for a walk around the lake? I want to make plans for when Mom gets here."

I'd forgotten her mother, whom I affectionately called Mama Hegler, was coming to visit the week of my birthday. It would be Lisa's mom's first visit to our new home. Lisa wanted to make the week-long visit special. We both looked forward to her mom getting to spend time with the dogs too.

Riley usually ran ahead of us on our walks. She liked to scout things out by sniffing, then run another fifty feet ahead and repeat the sniffing drill. She could have been a DEA dog. Zoe's pattern of stalking us from a hundred feet behind continued. Wrigley always walked a little behind me. I stopped halfway to the bench and let him pass me. He continued walking, choosing to follow Lisa. After fifteen feet he stopped, turned, and looked back at me. I think he was deciding whom he wanted to follow.

"What are you doing?" Lisa asked me.

"Checking out your ass," I replied.

"Will you be serious for one minute? You know I'm working every day next week so I can take time off when Mom's here. Can we discuss what we're going to do, please?"

"Have you noticed Wrigley acting different lately?" I asked, instead of answering her.

"Did you hear one thing I just told you?" Lisa was obviously frustrated with me. My first clue was her clenched teeth and barely moving lips when she spoke and it wasn't that cold out.

"I'm sorry," I said, still distracted. "I'm just afraid something may be wrong with Wrigley again."

Lisa stopped walking. "You're so cute the way you worry about him. I never would've pictured you as the overprotective parent, Paul. It's a sweet side of you." She watched Riley running back towards us and Wrigley walking back towards me and studied his movement.

"I've noticed Riley wanting to go out, and Wrigley's wanted to stay in and lie on the sofa. I thought he was just tired. He doesn't seem to be raising his head as high as he used to though. I haven't noticed him dragging his left rear paw, but now that you mention it, I guess he has been favoring it more. I agree he's definitely been less active," she said, closing her observations.

"We can talk about Mom's stay later. Let's head back. I'm getting cold and I think Wrigley wants to go back too." Lisa watched Wrigley more closely on the way home. "Hey Paul, I see what you mean about that leg. He is dragging it behind a little bit. Poor fella," she said, placing her hands on him.

I pulled out a leash to rein in Riley. She'd run back to us once and then away for another scouting mission.

"Go ahead, Lisa. I'll meet you back at the house. Riley needs some more time," I told her. The contrast between Wrigley and Riley walking or running was extreme. I had worried about him since his shot, but something was changing gradually with him and it wasn't positive.

Three days passed and Wrigley's condition worsened. He was not lifting his head higher than the line of his back. He was having a difficult time getting on and off the sofa. He was only eating half the food in his bowl. I had to start picking it up after he'd walk away because Riley started thinking it was hers. On the day Wrigley chose only to go outside to complete his business, I called Dr. Shiller's office and set up an appointment. I should have called sooner, but was holding out hope things would change on their own.

JoAnn, Dr. Shiller's receptionist, loved Wrigley. She liked me and Lisa too because we had worked hard to help Wrigley get better. JoAnn fit Wrigley's appointment between two others so he could be seen as soon as possible. She told us a lot of people would've put their pet down if it had experienced an episode like Wrigley's after his shot.

I remember her telling us during a previous appointment, "Some people simply don't want to deal with a pet that requires anything other than feeding and walking. It pisses me off. Those kind of people don't deserve the company of a dog." She was passionate and a true animal lover. Her own dog laid comfortably behind the receptionist desk in the clinic's waiting area on the days she worked.

The following morning I called for Wrigley to meet me at the door. He staggered in, barely raising his head when I knelt down to pet him. Lisa took the morning off so she could go to the vet with me and Wrigley. Riley sprinted to the kitchen door as we all headed out to the breezeway.

"No girl. You're staying here. No go. Stay," I told her. That was my code-speak for the dogs. "No go, stay," meant "you're not going along for the ride." At least I knew what it meant.

"Why can't Riley come with us?" Lisa asked.

"I only want to deal with Wrigley right now. She'll make it a pain getting Wrigley in and out of the SUV if she comes along. Why don't you give her that huge new bone that you have in your office. That'll keep her so occupied she won't even know we're gone."

Lisa called Riley to the sofa and unwrapped the bone. Riley's tail banged against the living room wall as she stood tall and steady on the sofa cushions. When Lisa turned to leave, without hesitation Riley dropped the bone on the floor, buzzed by Lisa and was waiting for her at the door.

Lisa bent over and hugged her, "You're going to be fine, girl. We'll be back with Wrigley before you know it, sweetie. Go chew your treat. I have to go, baby. I love you, Riley. You'll be ok."

When Lisa got in the Yukon, she had tears in her eyes.

"What's wrong?" I asked.

"This is the first time since we brought her home four months ago that she's been left alone without Wrigley or one of us. I feel bad leaving her. She knows something's wrong," Lisa replied.

"Did you read her tail? Was she wagging her concern? Is that what it told you?"

Lisa gave me a haughty look that confirmed the timing of my joke was not welcome.

At the vet's office, when I lifted Wrigley out of the Yukon, I strained my back. I've had back problems for years from manipulating extension ladders up to forty feet tall. Sometimes when I picked Wrigley up it aggravated his hurt leg and he'd twist his body. That's what caused the worst pressure and pain with my spine. I was paying a physical price for carting around our hundred-pound Great Dane puppy.

I stretched after setting Wrigley down. I tried to release the pressure that built up without success.

"Remind me to call Dr. Blabey when we get home, Lisa. My back's killing me." Dr. Blabey was my chiropractor for the last fifteen years.

"Okay, I will. Do you know Wrigley's peeing on your pants right now?" Lisa said, walking away, not trying to hide her laughter. "He thinks you're a fire hydrant, Paul."

She thought she was hilarious, I'm guessing.

I was pissed off about being pissed on. "Damn it, Wrigley!" I scolded him.

He didn't lift his head up, but he raised his eyes as high as he could manage and looked at me. I think he was trying to say he was sorry. I felt like shit for yelling at him.

"It's okay, boy. You're a good dog. I'm sorry I yelled. You're not feeling well are you, buddy? It's okay, Wrig," I reassured him as we walked slowly towards the clinic.

The waiting area was completely full. JoAnn ushered me and Wrigley into an exam room off the lobby. Lisa was already sitting inside waiting for us.

JoAnn was starting to take Wrigley out to the scale in the hallway but stopped in her tracks.

"We weighed you last time big guy. You look about the same weight, minus a few." She let go of Wrigley's leash. It was a good decision.

Animal hospitals, clinics and vet offices were obsessed with recording Wrigley's weight each time he had an appointment, even if he'd just been there a day or week earlier. Wrigley had an equal obsession. He could not stand being weighed and did everything in his power to avoid helping in the process of being weighed. The drama that ensued when they tried to weigh Wrigley was ridiculous. He'd go into his "frozen prehistoric animal, found in the Arctic" mode.

His dead-weight act required two or more people to lift him onto the scale. If they were successful in getting him on, he'd drop down immediately and spread his legs so one leg or another would be off the scale. For a dog that struggled to walk, he could give a yoga instructor a lesson or two in body contortions when he wanted to.

Wrigley's size prevented him from being examined on a table. Dr. Shiller knelt down on the floor. He pet him and gently rubbed his neck for a minute, then placed his hands on Wrigley's left rear leg, slowly pulling it forward.

Wrigley showed his teeth and growled before Dr. Shiller could extend the leg completely straight out. I'd never seen Wrigley behave like that. It was the first time I'd seen all his teeth and heard that deep growl. I realized how scary and dangerous Wrigley could be when he was in pain, feeling vulnerable.

"I'm sorry, Wrigley. You didn't like that, did you?" Dr. Shiller soothed him with words and gentle petting.

After releasing Wrigley's leg he placed his hands on Wrigley's neck and pressed his thumb and finger down each indentation of Wrigley's spine.

"Did you notice when I extended his leg how his paw cupped or collapsed as if it's unhinged? I'm afraid this may be more than just an orthopedic issue. This may also be a neurological problem," he informed us.

"His coat's thinning. Has he been scratching a lot lately?" Dr. Shiller asked us.

"Yeah, now that you mention it. He's been licking himself a lot," I replied.

"He's losing patches of hair. Stress can cause that, but I think he may have mange," he speculated.

I didn't know what mange was, but it turned out Wrigley had it. He'd been licking, scratching and biting his own flesh trying to relieve the discomfort from the parasite eating his skin. It's a microbe that normally cohabitates on an animal's fur. However, a compromised immune system allows the parasite to take over and start eating the animal's flesh. It was a disgusting process to hear about, especially knowing it was happening with our puppy.

Dr. Shiller prescribed an antibiotic, believing Wrigley had an infection. He also prescribed a pain killer with codeine because it was obvious Wrigley was in pain when he walked. The mange medication was fairly toxic, strong enough to be used on cows and pigs to stop hoof disease.

Dr. Shiller identified two of the medications that could make Wrigley lethargic. The combination of all three completely wiped him out. The meds also suppressed his appetite. Our puppy looked like hell. He was losing his hair, losing weight and what bothered me most, his happy puppy spirit. The only time he went out was to pee or poop.

He couldn't jump up onto or off the sofa three days after our appointment with Dr. Shiller. Wrigley was sleeping on the bed we bought for Riley and she was now sleeping in Wrigley's favorite spot on the sofa.

If that didn't pull at our hearts enough, Riley began avoiding him. Cassie was the only animal in the house that would get close to Wrigley. The medications left him practically comatose. It was heartbreaking to see him. I knew his life sucked, and I was beginning to feel the same way about mine. It felt like we just couldn't catch a break, not even for a few months.

I began signaling for Riley to meet me in the basement when it was time to go outside. I felt sick to my stomach watching Wrigley follow us with his eyes when we went out the breezeway door without him. It felt like punishment to me, leaving him behind. Not that he'd done anything wrong but have bad luck.

Wrigley's behavior reminded me of how he was in that cage in the animal hospital after his vaccine reaction. I felt guilty because I preferred the company of Riley over his. She was full of life and energy, representing the dog I had hoped to bring home when we first got Wrigley. I didn't have the same passion about saving him this time because of Riley.

It was selfish on my part, but I wondered if he'd be better off if we stopped trying to help him and let him go. Deep down I thought and wanted to believe I'd be better off.

I had an appointment with Dr. Blabey, my chiropractor, the next day, at three-thirty. Wrigley's appointment with an orthopedist was eleven days away. Dr. Shiller thought the specialist would be able to pinpoint his issue, whether it was singularly orthopedic or neurological, or both.

That night I asked Lisa something that I wished I hadn't.

"If the orthopedist says Wrigley has some terrible bone disease or chronic illness, I'm thinking we need to be prepared or open to the possibility of exploring that Wrigley may be better off by us making a decision that would allow him to stop suffering and being in pain all the time. You know what I mean?" I had dragged the question on so long its meaning was probably lost behind my nerves and fear.

The gravity of what I'd said didn't escape Lisa.

"You want to put him down? I'm not having this conversation. I don't believe you. God, Paul. What's gotten in to you? Wrigley's part of our family. Lord, I hope I never get sick, and you have to make decisions for me." She picked up her book and left the room, allowing me to contemplate what I'd just proposed.

It felt wrong, but I wanted my old life back. Parents endure hardship and heartbreak because they love their kids and that's what you do. But Wrigley was a dog, not my blood, not my son. He was a nine-month-old sick Great Dane puppy that was sucking up my emotional energy and stealing my freedom.

I wanted to push a button and have a "do over." We'd be fine with Riley, right? That's what I told myself and for that, I felt guilt and shame, but those feelings only added to my angst and misery.

Chapter 10

Tail of an Unscheduled Patient

My paint crew painted someone's living room the wrong color. It wasn't the kind of phone call I needed at the time. The customer demanded to meet with me at four, which meant I'd have to cancel my chiropractor appointment. I called the chiropractor's office hoping for an earlier appointment because my back was killing me.

My cell phone had a weak signal when I called.

"I'm sorry. I'm having trouble hearing you. Who's the appointment for?" Patty, the chiropractor's receptionist, asked.

"Wrigley Sullivan, it was scheduled for today at three. I wanted to come in earlier if possible. Otherwise I'll need to cancel," I told her.

"I'm not finding a Wrigley in the system," she told me.

I started laughing. "I'm sorry, it's Paul Sullivan, not Wrigley."

I'd made so many appointments for Wrigley in the last few weeks his name was on the tip of my tongue. I continued chuckling at myself while Patty squeezed an extra appointment in between two patients scheduled before lunch at eleven-thirty.

I let her know my back was thankful for the accommodation.

I grabbed my sunglasses, keys and wallet. Wrigley's leash, which hadn't been used in days, was hanging next to the breezeway door. "Wrigley. Come. Ride. Now," I said loudly. It might not be my best idea, but I wanted the chiropractor to take a look at Wrigley.

Riley responded immediately to my voice and met me in seconds. Wrigley was much slower, but he eventually arrived at the door.

"Sorry, girl. This ride's only for Wrigley," I told her, petting her head softly.

When we arrived at Dr. Blabey's office I held the door open and waited while Wrigley hobbled in. His back was humped as he dragged his left rear leg over the carpet. His head hung low, and he looked as though he could have fallen forward at any moment.

Patty, behind the counter, saw Wrigley. "Is he okay?"

"I don't know. That's why he's here. This may be unorthodox, but do you think Dr. Blabey would mind taking a look at him?" I had no idea how she'd respond.

Patty glanced behind her, toward Dr. Blabey's private office, then looked at me, then Wrigley. "Take him to room number three. It's probably best if he's not in the waiting area." Her primness implied we were potentially doing something wrong.

I understood her hesitancy, but I was desperate. I couldn't stand seeing Wrigley in pain any longer. It was slowly killing my spirit as well as his.

In the room, Wrigley lay down on his left side against the apparatus I'd be lying on while Dr. Blabey did his magic cracking my neck and body. He called it manipulating, but it sounded like cracking to me.

It was five minutes before the master manipulator came in.

"What do we have here?" Dr. Blabey asked, eyeballing the ninety-pound Great Dane lying flat on his exam room floor.

I studied his face, trying to assess his reaction. He remained calm, his usual Zen-like manner at the fore.

"Wrigley is...not doing very well," I started. "It'll be another week before he can see a specialist. Our vet thinks his problems may be neurological. I was hoping you'd be willing to take a look at him in case it's orthopedic in nature. Maybe try a few manipulations? He's in a lot of pain, even though he's on medication," I explained.

"I can do that. Sure. Is he friendly?"

"Yes." I responded, relieved he'd agreed to examine him.

"I'm always interested in challenging new cases." Dr. Blabey smiled and then knelt down next to Wrigley, laying both hands lightly on his skinny body. He rested them there for over a minute without moving them.

Wrigley's eyes followed his every move.

After a short time Wrigley allowed his eyes to close and fell asleep. I knew he was relaxed when he started snoring.

Dr. Blabey stretched Wrigley's right leg, extending it, and found its flexibility within a normal range. "His upper hindquarter on this right side is overcompensating for his weaker left side," he pointed out.

"Can you help me move him over onto his other side?"

Wrigley didn't appreciate the interruption of his peaceful slumber. He raised his head when Dr. Blabey extended his weak, slighter, left rear leg.

Without growling, Wrigley flashed his teeth, jerking his leg back toward his body when the leg crossed over his pain threshold. He let out a screeching yelp, then growled, clearly letting Dr. Blabey know it was time to "stop."

"Easy, Wrigley," I said, holding him in place. "It's okay, boy."

Dr. Blabey gave Wrigley time to calm down, which didn't take long. He then pressed his index and middle fingers down Wrigley's neck. He followed the path into each indentation of Wrigley's spine, locating pressure points and working down his spinal column slowly.

After a few minutes, Wrigley sighed and exhaled as he relaxed. He fell back into a deep sleep, quietly releasing soft-sounding, long, smelly farts.

"Hear that? When pressure's released, it feels good." Dr. Blabey explained.

"I thought you were asking me if I heard him farting at first." For the second time that day I was overcome by laughter. It felt good.

"Open that window behind you, would you? My next patient may fall over after walking in here. I should have asked you to open it earlier, but I wasn't sure who was doing the farting," Dr. Blabey joked.

I overheard his receptionist explaining to another patient in the adjacent examining room that the doctor was running behind with a "new" patient.

Dr. Blabey heard her too. "I'd better focus on you for few minutes," he told me. "Time got away from us with this big boy."

He motioned for me to get on the table. Dr. Blabey worked on my back. Wrigley didn't budge, but he continued sleeping and expelling gas. Dr. Blabey was a good guy, actually shuffling around Wrigley, trying not to disturb his blissful rest. Before leaving me and Wrigley, Dr. Blabey gave me a concise assessment.

"His issue begins at his neck. I was afraid to manipulate it without knowing exactly what's going on there. You'll need to get x-rays or an MRI. I provided some relief for him today. I'll need to see you again in three to five days. You're almost as tight as your dog," he said, exiting quickly.

I rattled Wrigley's leash, signaling to him that it was time to leave. He bounced up, walking out of the room ahead of me. I noticed he was putting more weight on his left rear leg and had a slight spring in his step. His head was held higher than it had been in three weeks as we walked out of the office.

I was dumbfounded and excited by the immediate change in his gait. I couldn't wait to tell Lisa.

When I told Lisa the story of how Wrigley used my appointment with Dr. Blabey, she kept repeating, "You did not. Tell me you didn't. This is a bad joke." She sounded quite unable to decide whether to be embarrassed by my audacity or proud of me for it.

I was jazzed, finding sudden hope that Wrigley might have a chance of getting better. He was a different dog walking out of that place.

"You are one crazy man, Paul Sullivan," Lisa told me. "I'm glad he's doing better. I should be home on time. We can talk then. I love you. Bye." Her work in the hospital called her attention away, but I knew she was happy with the news.

Chapter 11

Easy Come, Easy Go

My excitement and optimism regarding Wrigley's health evaporated rapidly. His improvement was too short-lived. He completely stopped eating within three days of our visit to the chiropractor. His ribcage stood out now. Mange had claimed large patches of his fur. He appeared to be almost too weak to scratch.

The antibiotic and mange medications weren't helping. I'm not sure the pain medication was either.

Dr. Shiller advised me to double Wrigley's pain medication dosage.

After that, Wrigley was barely conscious. Just trying to get him to drink water became a challenge. I had to hold him up when he went outside. Even Cassie stopped going near him. Riley was avoiding Wrigley too. She even stopped sleeping in the living room.

My puppy, my companion, my friend, was wasting away on the dog bed in the dining room. My wish for an easier life, without the hassles of a sick dog, were becoming a crisis of a broken heart, his and mine. Wrigley was dying. All his hope, awareness and love were disappearing in front of our eyes.

"Lisa, we need to talk about Wrigley," I told her after she came home late from work that night. She was tired and resistant, but I couldn't stand by any longer without addressing the reality of the situation. "Honey, it's gone on too long. This can't be about us. We need to keep it about him. He can barely go out to pee. Don't make me the bad guy here. We need to figure out what we're going to do. He can't live like this. Shit, we can't live like this. I know I can't."

Lisa refused to discuss ending Wrigley's life. "He came to us for a reason, Paul. I'm not ready to write him off like you are."

"That's so unfair, Lisa. I've spent the last seven months with him. I love him, and I also know him. He's miserable. It's killing me to see him like this."

Lisa started sobbing, overwhelmed. Her raw pain scared me. I didn't know what to do. I'd felt that way one other time with Lisa. It was one of the most painful experiences I'd ever known in my life. The person I loved most needed my comfort, my love, and I had nothing to offer then, much as I felt now.

Two years earlier, in late August, Lisa and I had rented a beach house in the little town of Eastham, on Cape Cod. I wanted the vacation to help both of us forget about all the baby stuff we had been immersed in. We had eaten a nice dinner that night and had too much to drink. When we got back we went straight to bed, and I wanted to make love. It was the first time in a long time it felt natural, not planned. I simply wanted to be with Lisa.

Lisa was at a different place. "I'm tired," she said. "Let's go to sleep. You can play 'minute man' in the morning, okay?" That was the term we used when trying to get pregnant during a busy work week.

I'm sure it was the alcohol and pent-up frustration, but I said a terrible thing to Lisa that night. I regret it to this day.

"Do you even remember how to make love? I'm fucking tired of our sex, always attached with a baby agenda," I screamed.

I'll never forget her face. I may as well have slapped her.

Lisa pulled half the covers off the bed and ran into the bathroom, slamming the door. When I opened it, she was shaking and sobbing, curled up in the fetal position.

"Get out! *Get out!* Leave me alone," she screamed, kicking the door shut with her foot.

I stood outside the bathroom door listening to her cry. I wanted to run away. I wanted my old single life back. I didn't want to be me or have anything to do with the man who had shouted those words. I should have said I was sorry and hugged her.

Instead, I went into the kitchen and filled my wine glass to the top. From another world away, she shrieked, "You don't understand! *I'm never going to have a baby.*"

I slid the door open from the family room and stepped out to the deck, overlooking the ocean. I could still hear Lisa struggling to breathe while crying. I slid the door shut.

I sat alone under the clear New England sky. I don't think I'd ever seen that many stars before. The late summer air was chilly. My fingers were cold from holding onto my wine glass. I watched as a streak of light, a falling star, streamed across the horizon, disappearing in the darkness over the ocean. It was beautiful. I was not.

Maybe I was smarter now than I was then, or maybe it was just easier to share my own grief. "Lisa, I love you, and I love Wrigley too. But we can't ignore what is happening. It's not fair to him or us. We need to be on the same page. Please."

My heartfelt plea failed to reach her. Lisa wasn't willing to imagine our life without Wrigley. I didn't know what to do.

The next morning I called Amy, our marriage counselor. The last time we'd seen her we had just moved into the new house. We had owned Wrigley for maybe a week or two. Because Amy shared our love of dogs, she invited us to bring Wrigley along to our last session.

During that appointment, our ten-week-old puppy sat on Amy's lap without moving for fifty minutes. Amy rubbed behind his ears and pet him while we brought our therapeutic relationship to an end. That was seven months ago. It seemed much longer.

Ironically, this time we needed to see Amy about ending our puppy's life, not about having a baby.

Lisa and I knew what difficult sessions were like because we'd been through several. One in particular stood out. We had just been informed that the single egg from our last in vitro fertilization cycle wasn't viable. I was tired of our life revolving around trying to have a baby. Lisa, not willing to give up, wanted us to explore using surrogate eggs to be fertilized with my sperm and then implanted in Lisa.

Our savings were already depleted. We'd spent over $100,000, and the surrogate program was $30,000 if everything went smoothly. I had refused to review the biographies of potential egg donors at the infertility clinic. Lisa was angry with me.

"How can you quit now after everything we've been through?" she had demanded. "I promise, this is the last thing I'll ask you to do."

"I can't. I don't have the energy for anything else. What's the point of having a baby if we don't have a relationship? Can't you see I'm done?"

I'd never been as honest with myself or Lisa in a session as I was that day. I remember saying, "I don't have any hope for us."

"Lisa," Amy said, "did you hear Paul? He doesn't have anything more to give to you or your relationship right now. You're going to have to carry the load until that changes. Can you do that?"

I was shocked. You can do that? Just let someone else carry the load for a while? The weight of the world lifted off my shoulders.

When I told Lisa about setting up an appointment with Amy about Wrigley, she was upset that I'd made the appointment without checking with her first. "We can't run to Amy every time we have a disagreement, Paul."

"I can't go alone, Lisa. It's called couples therapy for a reason. You won't talk with me about Wrigley. We need help."

She finally agreed to go.

Amy had offered us an appointment on the same day and time we'd met with her for three years. Thursday, at three-thirty. Our appointment was in six days.

Chapter 12

The Unexpected

As we were navigating the Wrigley situation, Lisa and I began to notice that Riley was acting strangely. We attributed her behavior to Wrigley's illness, assuming she was depressed. She stopped eating as much and began to take longer to do her business. She'd hold her position to poop for several minutes, but achieve no results.

Lisa and I took her to Dr. Shiller's on Saturday. It was odd leaving Wrigley, who was so sick, back at the house. He barely lifted his head as we all departed. His gaze broke my heart. His appointment with the orthopedic specialist was still a week away, and I honestly wondered if he'd live that long. There was a part of me that wanted our puppy to pass away in his sleep. Then Lisa and I wouldn't have to make the decision.

Dr. Shiller listened to Riley's heart and stomach with his stethoscope. "Heart sounds strong. Her belly's rumbling. Probably something she ate."

He gave us some medication to cover a GI issue that would settle Riley's stomach and instructed us to give her an antacid with dinner. "If she isn't eating or going to the bathroom normally by Sunday, bring her back Monday morning and we'll run some tests," he instructed us.

Great. Now our healthy dog needed testing.

At least Riley jumped into the back of the Yukon ready to head home after the appointment. She was completely different from Wrigley during car rides. She pressed her snout against the glass and soaked in the sights.

When we returned home, Wrigley met us at the door.

"Wrigley," Lisa said, "You feeling better, buddy?"

She watched as Wrigley dragged himself out to the breezeway. He didn't make it to the end of the walkway before he started to pee. The stream of urine collided and splashed onto his front left paw because of his awkward stance. I think Lisa saw, for the first time, what I'd been telling her for over a week.

Wrigley was a very sick dog. I didn't say anything. I didn't need to.

"I'll watch him," I said. It was obvious she was caught off-guard by what she'd just seen.

I called for Wrigley to meet me on the front lawn. That constituted a long walk for him now.

Our neighbor, Greg, was walking down the sidewalk toward our house with his Golden Retriever, Emma. She was the first dog Wrigley had met in our neighborhood. He loved Emma. As Greg approached, Wrigley's pal Emma pulled back, refusing to get too close.

Sadly, Wrigley reciprocated the sentiment by showing Emma little recognition and zero interest.

"My God, Paul, what happened? He doesn't look like the same dog," Greg said. "I heard he'd relapsed, but I can't believe how much he's deteriorated since I saw him last. It's only been two weeks!"

I took Wrigley inside the house and went back outside to speak with Greg. He believed he had some possible help for Wrigley.

I was open to any suggestions at that point.

"You've heard me speak of Hoss, our old dog, the Greyhound we rescued?" Greg asked.

I'd never met Hoss but felt like I had because Greg spoke of him often. Loss is a circular process. A new loss stirs up old feelings from previous losses. Countless times in bereavement groups, members spoke of losses from twenty years earlier. It didn't mean the loss wasn't resolved, but it was worthy of being revisited from a different place in that person's life.

I couldn't help but think Greg sensed we'd be losing Wrigley soon, and he wanted to try to make things easier for us. When my mom died, the most helpful people were those who'd already experienced a traumatic loss in their life. They provided comfort, letting me know I'd get through it and be okay.

"I heard you took Wrigley to your chiropractor. When I heard that, I figured you'd be open to other alternative treatments for helping Wrigley," he said, piquing my curiosity.

"What kind of alternative medicine are you talking about? It's not witchcraft or voodoo is it?" I was half-joking, not sure where he was headed.

"No, nothing like that. I met a lady who helped Hoss with his pain at the end. She's an American Indian with special healing powers. I spoke with her about Wrigley. She'd happily meet with you if you're interested. You don't need to decide now, but here's her number if you want to call. When I told her about Wrigley not too long ago, she mentioned that she has successfully helped other dogs with similar conditions. You know, allergic reactions from a shot."

I didn't commit, but thanked him for the referral. When I walked in the living room, Lisa was sitting close to Wrigley, encouraging Riley to come over to them.

"I know this sounds crazy, but would you be open to a spiritual animal healer coming out to help Wrigley?" I asked.

"You're not serious, are you?" From the look on my face, she gathered I wasn't kidding.

"I'm sorry, sweetie. I didn't mean to make fun. What does a spiritual animal healer do? Is this what Greg was talking to you about?"

I couldn't figure out which question to answer. "Forget it. It's probably a waste of time," I muttered.

Lisa stood up and hugged me. "I'm glad you're willing to try anything to help him. You were so excited after taking him to Dr. Blabey's. I knew you didn't want to give up on him, and I know it's been especially hard for you. I didn't understand how much time you have to spend with him, Paul. Honestly, the whole Indian healer thing is pretty out there, but why don't you call and see what your instincts say? Maybe we'll at least meet once. After all, information is power." Lisa rubbed my shoulders. I knew her agreeing to Wrigley being treated by an American Indian spiritual animal healer was a huge stretch, so I immediately picked up my cell phone and dialed.

The phone rang over eight times without a voice mail kicking in. I was about to hang up when I heard a soft, throaty voice say, "This Warm Breeze. May I help you?"

In a short conversation, Warm Breeze explained what Lisa and I could expect from her visit. She requested that Lisa and all the animals or "living beings" residing in our home be present when she arrived.

She wanted to make an "energy assessment" of our home. I was surprised when she offered to meet Tuesday, only two days away.

Lisa had already scheduled time off for Thursday's appointment with Amy for our counseling session. She wouldn't be happy taking Tuesday off as well because her mom was arriving Saturday.

"Paul, now I'll have to work Friday. That doesn't give me time to get things ready for Mom! Why do I need to be here anyway? This is sounding like a lot of hocus-pocus." She gave a huge sigh. "Okay, okay, I'll commit to meet with Big Wind for one hour, but the rest of the day is mine."

"Her name is Warm Breeze, not Big Wind."

"Warm Breeze, Big Wind, what's the difference?" She wasn't smiling when she said it either.

That night I put the trash out for Monday's pickup. When I came back in I found Lisa sitting on Wrigley's sofa with Riley's head resting on her lap.

"Have you noticed Riley hasn't jumped up once today when you or I came in? She's not feeling well. Will you take her back to Dr. Shiller's tomorrow morning? I'm worried about her."

Was it too much to have one day that wasn't interrupted by a vet appointment? I had six painting contracts waiting to be sent out and my crew was starting a new job, requiring me to be on site at seven in the morning. Nevertheless, I grudgingly agreed to take Riley to see Dr. Shiller. The appointment would have to wait until the afternoon because there was no way to reschedule everything else.

As it turned out, JoAnn, the vet's assistant, didn't have an appointment available until in the afternoon anyway. If I had needed to get Wrigley in, I could have picked the time, because he was a special case. I'm pretty sure JoAnn had Dr. Shiller's approval to give Wrigley priority. He had a special survival status that Riley hadn't earned.

I returned home at two-thirty to take Riley to the vet. Both dogs met me at the door. That hadn't occurred in some time. I let Wrigley out to pee and called Riley, pointing for her to jump into the Yukon.

She refused, and I had to lift her up like I did for Wrigley. She felt bloated when my arms wrapped around her body. Her eyes didn't have their normal energetic sparkle. Neither dog had touched their food this morning.

I had read that it wasn't uncommon for animals to take on matching symptoms when their owners were ill. Depression was also common when an animal companion was sick. Poor Riley. She loved

Wrigley and missed her playing companion. Lisa and I had focused so much attention on Wrigley, we'd neglected giving her normal amounts of attention.

Before I took Wrigley back into the house, he swaggered over to the SUV and stared. Riley was lying on the dog bed, not standing, so he couldn't see her. He raised his head higher than I'd seen in some time, and let out a short bark, a deep coughing sound. Strange.

I urged him back inside and spotted all three cats. I hadn't seen them all at one time in a few weeks. They'd all been MIA since Wrigley became ill again. I said farewell, using all three of their names, as I placed a blanket over Wrigley and headed out the door.

On the way to the vet Lisa called.

"I'm taking her now. I promise to call you on my way back home," I told her.

I had to lift Riley out of the SUV. She walked slowly towards the doors. Her behavior was eerily similar to Wrigley's. Well, maybe she was constipated, a side effect of the medication she'd taken.

I wasn't overly concerned, except when I looked into her eyes and saw the sadness.

Dr. Shiller didn't waste time with his normal gregarious pleasantries. He immediately felt Riley's belly after entering the room. There was resistance, caused by pressure.

The vet looked at me. "Nothing's getting through."

"JoAnn," Dr. Shiller yelled. "I need your help. Set things up for an enema." He was in full doctor mode. He asked me to leave the room and he shut the door behind me.

After a few minutes JoAnn came back out of the exam room with Riley attached to her leash.

"This doesn't take long. Stay clear, coming through," she advised lightly.

I held the door open for Riley and JoAnn. They headed straight for a grassy area off the parking lot.

We chatted about the welcome warm April weather and speculated about whether we would get anymore snow.

Five minutes passed, but nothing happened. After a few more minutes JoAnn handed me Riley's leash. "Will you hold her? I need to speak with Dr. Shiller." She nearly ran back into the clinic.

"Is everything okay?" I shouted just before she made it inside.

"Just stay with her. I'll be back in a minute." She disappeared through a side door of the building.

I bent down and put my face in front of Riley's. "You're a sweet girl, Riley. Don't worry. Once you're cleared out, you're going to feel much better." I pet her behind her ears with both of my hands.

In return she looked at me, almost apologetically. There was something missing from her, but I didn't know what it was.

"Paul! Bring Riley, hurry. Dr. Shiller needs to see her," JoAnn yelled from the side door.

I'd barely gotten Riley into the exam room when Dr. Shiller came in. He grabbed Riley's leash from me and positioned Riley flat on her left side. Without assistance from JoAnn, he jabbed a long needle into Riley's belly and pulled back on the syringe, collecting fluid directly from her abdomen. Just as quickly, he grabbed another needle and drew blood from her leg.

"I'll be back in a few minutes. I need to check these in the lab." He rushed out of the room.

Riley never moved from the cold tile floor. I sat down with her and stroked her face softly. Her belly was bigger than when we'd arrived. Riley let out a soft sigh as I rubbed behind her ears and kissed her snout.

"What's going on, girl? All this vet stuff is Wrigley's game, not yours." My concern ratcheted up the longer I waited for Dr. Shiller to return.

When he finally came back, he was flushed, upset and out of breath.

"I'm sorry," he said. "I can't believe with everything you and Lisa have been through I have to tell you this. Riley has peritonitis. I can't provide what she needs here. I'll call South Paws Emergency Animal Hospital and tell them you're on the way. Hopefully they can do something for her." His voice trailed off miserably.

JoAnn handed me Riley's leash, "Go. Every minute counts."

The severity of the situation hit me. I knew the answer before I asked, "This is a life or death situation?"

"Yes. It often is," Dr Shiller responded. "Now hurry, and get there safely."

Chapter 13

The Life of Riley

Riley's appointment had pushed us into rush hour. Depending on traffic, the drive from Great Falls to Fairfax could take up to an hour. A not-so-bright illegal u-turn almost caused a collision, but I pulled into South Paws Animal Hospital in forty-four minutes.

I'd paged Lisa on the way, but hadn't heard from her. I wanted to carry Riley into the hospital, but she yelped when I picked her up. We walked in slow motion into the five-story building.

The lady behind the long reception watched as we approached the counter. "I'm Paul Sullivan. Dr. Shiller said he'd..." I never had a chance to finish.

"He called." She picked up her phone and uttered a numbered code followed by, "Great Dane, female, main entrance."

Two guys appeared and had Riley on a gurney in no time. They wheeled her quickly through two electronic doors, leaving me staring at the closed doors, numb.

Normally I'd be congratulating myself about my record fast arrival, but all I could think of was that I wanted Lisa to be with me and wished she'd called me back.

The receptionist waved a clipboard in the air, trying to get my attention.

"Mr. Sullivan. Can you fill out these forms? Both sides, please. You can have a seat over there." Nearly every square inch of the huge room was decorated with paintings and sculptures of cats and dogs. The late afternoon sun slanted through large windows.

I sat down, took a deep breath, and exhaled. I told myself everything would be okay. Riley was a healthy and strong pup. Then I remembered Wrigley making the unusual effort to walk to the Yukon and barking goodbye. I stopped myself from going down that road. Riley was our healthy puppy. She'd be fine.

My phone rang at five forty-seven.

It was Lisa. "Did you mean to push 'urgent' when you paged me?"

"Yeah. I guess I should have pushed it a couple times," I replied.

"What's urgent? Is it Wrigley?"

"I'm in Fairfax, at South Paws Animal Hospital. I had to bring Riley here. I haven't spoken with anyone yet. Dr. Shiller said it was peritonitis."

"Peritonitis? What makes him think he's got that?" she asked, surprised.

"I don't know. I rushed out of there before I could ask any detailed questions. He said if I didn't get her here immediately she could die."

"I'm confused. You keep saying her. You mean him, Wrigley, right?" Lisa asked.

"No, I mean her, Riley, not Wrigley, Riley." I clarified.

"I don't believe this. Why does he think it's peritonitis?"

"They tried giving her an enema and it didn't work. Then they rushed her back inside. He looked at her gums, then drew fluid from her belly, which is totally bloated, by the way. You wouldn't believe how different she looks from this morning. She could barely walk on her own. After drawing blood, Dr. Shiller came back and said it was a life and death situation. Is that true?" I didn't have a clue what peritonitis was. I thought it was a dental issue.

When Lisa answered me, my heart sank. Her voice had the same methodical, calm delivery she used while explaining why my mom's surgery, her last chance of prolonging life from the pancreatic cancer, was aborted mid-procedure. I'm sure it was the voice Lisa used with family members of sick patients too. She was calm and matter-of-fact, but also soft and caring.

"Remember when your Uncle Timmy got sepsis? Your mom did too at the end. Peritonitis and sepsis are similar; relating to infection. It can be fatal if it's not caught in time," she explained.

I heard Lisa's pager going off as we spoke. The beeps got louder and longer with each set. The sound only made me more desperate. "I know you're busy, but I'm...pretty burned out on all this dog stuff. The hospital is off 495, the exit before Braddock Road. Will you leave? I don't want to be here alone when they come out with the diagnosis," I said.

"I know. I really appreciate you handling all the stuff. I've been paged three times while talking with you. It's crazy here, but I'll see what I can do." Her strong, confident voice broke. "I can't believe this is happening. I can't believe it's happening with Wrigley, I mean Riley." I could tell she was holding back from crying.

Lisa always said "information is power," but this was one time I was ambivalent about receiving information. We were already waiting for Wrigley's diagnosis. I wasn't ready for a bad one for Riley. Instead of relaxing me, talking with Lisa had increased my anxiety.

All too soon, I was called back to a small private conference room in the far corner of the waiting area. I don't remember the vet's name who spoke to me. He had a New York or Boston accent. I sat motionless and listened to him tell me terrible news about my dog, but this time it wasn't Wrigley...it was Riley.

"We don't have any great options. Riley's a very sick dog. Every ounce of fluid retained is worsening her condition and increasing her pain. In the hour and a half she's been here, she's retained an additional three liters of fluid. Her total retention now is ten liters. That's causing an immense amount of pressure. She's closing in on a critical point. You'll need to decide quickly how you want to proceed. I wish there was something else I could offer, but she's a very sick puppy," he explained.

My mind floated out of my body for a period as the vet explained procedures, potential costs and odds of success for saving Riley. I didn't understand half of what he was saying and I didn't bother asking any questions. One thing was crystal clear. Riley was dying.

I knew Lisa would want to save her, but the vet as much told me it was a mistake to try. She was too far gone. The procedure that might give her any chance required opening up her entire abdomen, cleaning it out and then hoping infection didn't take over again. The odds were against her. The procedure cost started at $6,000, and that was a conservative estimate.

We'd already spent over $10,000 on Wrigley with all his vet appointments, hospital visits, special diets and medications.

I couldn't believe I was being asked to make this choice with Riley. It would have been easier with Wrigley, but Riley was all the promise and hope that came with the good dog, the healthy dog. What did we have left if we lost her? We'd only have Wrigley, who was unable to get up onto or off a sofa by himself. He could barely eat a meal or pee without hitting his own leg.

Anger nearly consumed me. Where was Lisa?

This was bullshit, me sitting here alone, knowing she'd want to save Riley, and me knowing it was absolutely the wrong decision. I had to wonder if it was possible for me to survive with all this shit piled on top of me.

All that aside, I couldn't forget Riley's sad eyes and I knew she was suffering. She was a beautiful, loving animal. I couldn't imagine putting her through a horrible, hopeless surgery and more pain. It wasn't fair to her. It would be selfish on our part.

"I'm inclined to not go forward with any treatment to save her," I said. "But she's not just my dog. My wife will want to have a say too. She'll want to save her, and she'll want to talk with you. We have another dog, and he's sick too. This is going to be a huge loss for us, for her. I'd ask that you be as clear and honest with her as you were with me. Lisa's smart. She'll know what we need to do." I had to stop to wipe tears from my eyes.

"I understand," the vet said. "It's important you let me know as quickly as you can. She is in a great deal of distress," he emphasized again.

Over the phone, I shared everything the vet told me with Lisa, including Riley's poor prognosis and the level of pain she was experiencing.

Lisa kept saying, "I can't believe this. Not Riley. This isn't happening."

"We have to make a decision together and quickly, Lisa," I said. "She's at a critical point and our indecision is causing her more pain. Either we tell them to treat her, or," my voice cracked, and I stuttered, "or we need to put her down."

Lisa's sniffling was my only response. "I don't think we have a choice, Lisa. Honey, we need to let her go." My heart broke as I said those words.

"We're not putting her down. I love her too much. What about Wrigley? He needs her now. I need her. Tell them we want to save her," she told me.

"Lisa, you didn't see her. She's in pain. I want you to talk with the vet. I'll do what you want after you hear what he says, and if you still believe trying to save Riley is the right thing to do, I'll accept that decision."

I listened as the vet answered Lisa's questions. I knew when the vet said, "Probably a nine or ten," Lisa had asked the level of pain Riley was experiencing. I also knew his last answer was to the question, "What would you do if Riley was your dog, under these same conditions?"

The vet started, "Chances are she won't make it through surgery. Her condition is critical, which I know you understand. You can appreciate her chances of a reoccurring infection once she's flushed out. If that happens, the entire procedure is repeated, only increasing the chance of losing her on the table. I can't give you a percentage or guarantee. It's the worst thing she could have. The prognosis is never good with this kind of problem. It's expensive, too. A family tried saving their dog a year ago under similar circumstances. It cost $17,000, the dog suffered for six days and then died. I can't reiterate enough the pain Riley's experiencing." He handed me back my phone.

There was silence on Lisa's end. I waited for her to speak. She was crying uncontrollably. Tears rolled down my own face, but I tried to speak and cover up the sound of my choking at the same time.

I got it together enough to say, "Sweetie, what are we going to tell them? They're waiting."

I felt her pain and devastation. We'd shared so much of it together before.

The silence was worse than anything, so I babbled. "I love Riley too, honey. I know you have a special relationship with her. If you'd seen her, you wouldn't be struggling with the decision. She isn't like Wrigley after his shot. They're isn't any fight left in her."

"I know what we should do; need to do," she told me. "I just don't want to. I love her so much, Paul. She's our baby girl." Lisa got her crying under control. "I'm leaving now."

I wanted to be strong, but my sadness with the situation and hearing Lisa's pain made it impossible for me to continue holding back my own tears. It was a relief knowing I wasn't going to be alone though.

"Go ahead, tell them we're not going forward with the surgery, Paul. But please don't let them do anything with her before I get there. I want to hold her one last time. I want to say goodbye to our sweet baby girl."

Chapter 14

Reaching the Rainbow

I informed the vet we wouldn't be going forward with any treatment. He immediately administered Riley medication to alleviate her pain temporarily. Her body was now twice as bloated as it had been that morning.

It was eight forty-five in the evening by the time Lisa arrived at the animal hospital. Riley and I were waiting for her in the small conference room where I'd met with the vet.

I lay next to Riley, almost spooning with her on the throw carpet in the middle of the room. Riley raised her head when she saw Lisa, and her tail wagged twice before she dropped it back down on the floor. She never took her eyes off of Lisa, watching her lie down beside her, on the opposite side from me.

"Poor little, bug. Sweet Riley. I'm so sorry, baby. I'm so sorry." Tears flooded Lisa's eyes. She put one hand over Riley's body and took my hand with her other. "I'm sorry to you too, honey. I got crazy on the phone. I can't imagine what I put you through." She gently pulled my hand to her mouth and kissed it.

"It's not a call you expect to get. I might very well have responded the same way if I'd gotten the call from you. I'm glad you're here. Riley is too. Did you see she gave you a two-wag welcome when you came in?"

"Yeah, I did. I can't believe how bloated she is, Paul. I kissed her goodbye this morning, and she looked perfectly normal. I can see what you meant. It's easier being here with you, with her, knowing." Lisa never stopped holding either of us. I was so glad she was here.

The vet knocked at the door. "Sorry to interrupt. There are a few things I need to go over with you. First of all, please take as much time as you need. Riley's medicated and comfortable. I've already set up her IV lines, so let me know when you're ready. If you want to be here, I'll let you know what to expect."

We couldn't imagine letting her pass without us being with her. He went on.

"You'll see me push two separate injections through her IV. The first one will put her in a deep sleep. The second one will stop her breathing. The entire process will take about three minutes. She won't feel any pain, I promise." With that, he left us alone with Riley.

I thought the vet was very respectful and kind. It helped. I liked hearing Riley wouldn't be in any pain. I'd felt guilty for the time we took making our decision. We both stroked her body softly. Our four months with her filled our hearts like it was a lifetime. Sadly it was too short of one.

"We'll say goodbye to Wrigley for you baby," I said. Riley's eyes focused on me when I mentioned his name. "Cassie and Precious, maybe even Zoe will miss you too girl." I was able to smile as Lisa met my eyes. We continued caressing her and telling her how we loved her and how special she was and how lucky Wrigley and we were to have had her in our lives.

We said goodbye for forty-five minutes. Much of that time, Lisa had her head buried in Riley's bloated body. Finally, she looked up at me and said, "I know." We both did. We watched as the vet pushed the first injection. Riley lifted her head up, shifting slightly, while she looked at me, then Lisa. When she lay her head back down, she was at peace. She never took her eyes off Lisa.

When the second injection entered her body, she let out her last breath. That Monday night, Riley's heart stopped beating at nine fifty-two.

Lisa closed her eyes. Our Riley was gone.

Chapter 15

Personal Inventory

We were both physically and emotionally exhausted. On the way home, Lisa missed her exit for the Dulles Toll Road and ended up turning around in Great Falls. We probably should have driven home together, but she insisted she was fine. I know we were both glad I didn't have to take her back to the animal hospital in the morning for her car.

By the time I pulled into the driveway at eleven, Wrigley had been left alone for over eight hours. All the lights in the house were off. It was raining heavily. I reclined my seat and felt tears running down my face, seemingly in sync with the rain trailing down the windshield.

Lisa interrupted the moment of quiet time with a call, "I'm at McDonald's drive-thru. You want anything?"

I hadn't eaten since lunch, but wasn't hungry. "No, I'm good. I'm going to take Wrigley out. I'll feed him too. See you in a few."

I doubt Wrigley had any clue he'd been alone for eight hours. He walked through the breezeway to the front lawn and peed for a long time, maybe a full minute. No matter how sick he was, he never peed in the house, except for the time after the shot.

Wrigley despised the rain, shaking his head and floppy ears so vigorously the poor guy almost fell over. He quickly escaped to the cover of the breezeway and let me know he was ready to go back inside.

When he walked into the kitchen, he stopped at his bowl and ate. I was surprised. I wondered if he noticed Riley wasn't with me.

Lisa arrived at eleven thirty-five. She set a full McDonald's bag on the counter.

"I said I wasn't hungry," I repeated.

"It's mine. I couldn't eat it." She picked it up and threw it in the trash can. "How's Wrigley?"

"About the same. He ate some after we went out. I gave him his meds. He's on the dog bed. I thought about putting him on his sofa, but was afraid he might fall off. Figured we'd had enough drama. I'm going to bed, baby. I'm done in. You?" I kissed her forehead and gave her a lazy hug goodnight.

"No. I'm going to stay down here with Wrigley for a while. You okay?"

"Yeah, just wiped out." I headed up the stairs. I could hear her crying as I went into our bedroom. I considered going back down, but honestly had nothing left to offer her. I plopped onto the bed with my clothes still on and fell asleep.

At eight o'clock the next morning I was surprised to find Lisa next to me.

"I took today off," she reminded me.

I started to say, "I'll take Wrigley and Riley out." In fact, the only reason we'd been able to sleep in was because Riley was missing. She always bounded upstairs to wake us for their early morning walk.

It was the first time in a new day I'd realized what happened the night before was real.

I was still dressed from the night before, so I offered to take Wrigley out and make the coffee. Lisa usually woke up at four-thirty in the morning on work days. Sleeping until eight was like a vacation, but this morning it wasn't welcome time off.

"Hey, come back when you're done. Let's sleep together for a little longer, then go to breakfast, okay?" Lisa suggested.

I could see Wrigley waiting for me at the bottom of the stairs. I'd normally take both dogs out much earlier. I already missed Riley, and I hadn't even walked down the stairs yet.

Wrigley was overly curious and sniffed excessively everywhere he walked that morning. He struggled to investigate the entire front lawn and the side of the house too.

Lisa was already downstairs by the time I'd brought Wrigley back inside. She was feeding the cats.

"I thought I was coming back up so we could sleep some more?" I said.

"You were outside forever. I couldn't sleep anymore. Let's go to breakfast now. I'm actually hungry. But you're not wearing those same clothes! Change, please, just for me?"

At the restaurant, we both ordered omelets. I noticed Lisa ate as little as I did. We didn't talk about Riley. What was there to say?

The waitress came by, asking if there was anything wrong with our meals.

"Everything's fine. We'll take the check though. Thanks," I replied.

I didn't want to wait for the waitress to pick up my credit card. I started to get up to pay it when Lisa reached over the table and grabbed my hand.

"Can we talk for a minute?" she asked me.

Oh no. I didn't want to talk about anything that required being asked about being talked about. I needed a break from talking and decision making. I didn't want to be a grown-up right now. I wanted to pretend I was the same single guy who used to drive to Myrtle Beach during the week of March Madness, golf, watch basketball and stay out late drinking at the bars with my buddies. I wanted to be anywhere else that could take me away from the pain and hopelessness I was feeling.

"What are we going to do?" she asked me.

"Just because we didn't eat our food, I think we should still pay the bill," I said.

"Please don't joke with me right now, Paul. You know what I mean. What are we going to do with Wrigley? We both know something is seriously wrong with him. But with Riley being gone..." Lisa stopped, started tearing up, but continued. "Doesn't that change things?"

Hearing Riley's name jolted me. Twenty-four hours earlier I was planning where to eat lunch before taking Riley to Dr. Shiller's office for a follow-up appointment. I never saw her death coming. Wrigley's situation was completely different.

"Lisa, I don't want to sound cruel or cold, but I don't want to spend the next several years of my life caring for a sick, three-legged dog. Do you really want to do this right now? Is a twenty-four hour mourning period for Riley too much to ask? I can't do this now."

"Did you want me to take that up, or would like more coffee?" the waitress interrupted.

Lisa and I didn't look up.

The waitress disappeared without taking my credit card or filling our empty cups of coffee. Smart gal.

Lisa sighed. "I can't think about losing Wrigley right now. At least not without offering him a fighting chance."

"So this is how it feels to say, 'Did you hear one thing I just told you?'" I quipped.

"Paul Sullivan, I know you love Wrigley. I see how gentle and caring you are with him. You love him, and he loves you. I want to cry sometimes when you're encouraging him to do the simplest things. It makes me think about how great a father you'd be."

"Don't, please, tie that into this! I'm seriously overwhelmed enough right now," I nearly shouted. The couple sitting at the table next to us looked over.

I may have been gentle and caring with Wrigley, but my outward behavior was masking high levels of impatience and frustration. Would Lisa think I'd make such a wonderful dad if she knew I wanted my old life back without the hassles of taking care of anyone or answering to anybody and their needs? What if we'd had a Down Syndrome baby or a child with autism? Would I be a good parent, suffering for my child, giving him everything I had to give or would I resent the child all the time?

All my friends who had kids told me, "having a child changes everything." I wondered what kind of father I'd be based on my mixed feelings about Wrigley. I did love our puppy, but I loved what my old life represented too.

"You can be so sweet sometimes, Paul," Lisa continued. "I wish you'd let that side of yourself make decisions. We'll get through this. It's painful going home right now, knowing Riley won't be there. You heard the vet say what happened with her was the worst thing that could have happened and I accepted that. We know she didn't have a chance, but Wrigley does. I have no idea why this has all happened, and frankly I don't care. I'm not willing to quit on Wrigley. He's a fighter. He's proved that already. He's lucky too," she said.

"Really? Lucky?" My sarcasm slipped out.

"Yeah, because he ended up with us. He's lucky because we love him and believe in him. I do at least, and I'm pretty sure you do, but right now you can only think of yourself. You can always have a life alone Paul, and lock your heart away, and you'll be more miserable than you know. Things look better from far away."

Lisa had a way of tweaking my brain and heart simultaneously. I respected and disliked this insight at the same time. She was right though. If I had to review my single life clearly and honestly, there was an underlying loneliness. Lisa saw and knew things about me I didn't admit to myself. She always claimed she had married "a diamond in the rough."

"Paul. Are you listening?" she prodded. "I want us to be on the same page regarding Wrigley. Let's agree to give him a chance. That's all I'm asking."

"We can discuss this when we see Amy," I said, wanting to put off any further discussion. "What I need right now is a nap," I told her.

Lisa grabbed her purse and stood abruptly. "You and I both know we don't need Amy to help us with this. I know how you feel. I only hope you're able to be honest enough with yourself to make the right decision. Sometimes you can't change things Paul, but sometimes you can. But you have to have faith and believe it's possible. Wrigley deserves that. Please don't quit on him or me." She walked away without looking back.

Chapter 16

The Ringing of the Bell

Lisa and I both decided to take a nap when we got home from not eating breakfast. I took my naps seriously, removing my clothes and getting under the covers even if I'd only be lying down for twenty minutes. Lisa's napping, on the other hand, required magazines to read, watching TV or possibly a quick online purchase off her laptop before settling down.

I had reached that perfect spot of semi-consciousness, plunging into my deep nap mode when the doorbell rang, and rang and rang.

"Don't answer it. It's probably one of those window or siding people or someone trying to sell us firewood again," Lisa muttered.

I couldn't return to my blissful nap after being pulled abruptly awake, so I dressed and headed downstairs.

Wrigley was standing on his bed totally alert. His stance had nothing to do with protecting our home, but any sounds of ringing or beeps disturbed him. He'd been like that after staying overnight at the emergency animal hospital.

Wrigley watched curiously as I opened the front door.

A tall, slender woman, maybe forty-five years old with long auburn hair, wearing tight designer blue jeans and high leather boots extended her hand to shake mine.

"Paul?" she inquired.

Wrigley moved off his bed and stood behind me in the foyer. Despite struggling to stand in place because his left leg kept sliding out, he stayed long enough to get a closer look at the person who dared disturb him by ringing the bell.

Wrigley feared many things he didn't understand or trust; vacuums, brooms standing in the corner of a hallway or a book laying on his sofa cushion. The irrational fears usually led to flight.

In this case, he was immediately on guard with the person standing at our door, and I watched with amazement as he backed up without falling, using only his three good legs. He retreated to the distant safety of his bed in the dining room, his eyes never leaving the visitor.

"How handsome. That has to be Wrigley." The lady took a step into the house.

"May I help you?" I asked. I couldn't remember if she was a neighbor we'd met or what. I had no clue how she knew my name and Wrigley's as well. I blocked her path from further entry into our home. "Excuse me, but I have no idea who you are."

"I'm Warm Breeze. We talked last week. Your neighbor Greg referred me," she explained.

Everything that had happened with Riley the night before had caused me to forget our appointment with the American Indian spiritual healer. The timing really couldn't have been worse.

"Right. God, I'm sorry. We totally forgot. We should have called you. It's not a great time for us to meet. We lost Riley last night, Wrigley's half-sister."

"How terrible. Is she still missing or did she come back home?"

"She's not lost, she passed away. You know, dead." My voice caught as I said it out loud for the first time. I swallowed hard and my face flamed hot.

"Please accept my sincere condolences. I'm here at a time of great mourning. I understand if you want privacy during this painful period. I'll respect your wishes and we could meet some other time, or I'm willing to stay and share in your sadness. I know what it is like to lose an animal, a pet, a friend."

"Let me check with Lisa. Why don't you sit down in the living room. I'll be right back."

Lisa's take on it was one of karma. "Maybe there's a reason she's here today, Paul. Maybe she can help Wrigley. But I can only meet for an hour because I'm getting my hair cut at two."

I was dumbfounded by Lisa's willingness to meet. Frankly, I wasn't sure I had the necessary energy or much of a desire to talk with anyone right now, but she was already here, and Wrigley wasn't exactly on his way to a miraculous cure. Maybe she could help.

I was disappointed that Warm Breeze hadn't met any of my expectations of what an American Indian spiritual healer would look like. I had envisioned animal skins and a full headdress arranged with colorful feathers. Did my fantastical image make me a racist or simply a victim of Hollywood? Stupid expectations or not, Warm Breeze resembled my Irish Aunt Rita from Chicago more than an American Indian. I hoped Warm Breeze couldn't read my mind.

When Lisa came downstairs the surprised look on her face told me that she must have shared at least some of my silly expectations for Warm Breeze, but she merely smiled and introduced herself.

Wrigley watched Lisa, me and the healer talk in the living room from his bed in the dining room. Each time Warm Breeze spoke, he lifted his head and focused on her, letting out long sighs or yawns until she finished speaking.

Warm Breeze had requested that all living beings that resided in our home be present. After only ten minutes she was about to relay her findings, but I realized Zoe was outside.

"Wait, Zoe's not here," I exclaimed.

"Just ignore him," Lisa said. "Paul jokes a lot. Try not to laugh, it only encourages him."

Warm Breeze wasn't ardent about us all being present. Thankfully, she moved forward without me trying to find and bring Zoe inside.

"The warmth and positive energy in your home brings me comfort. My hope, my wish, is to help you find even deeper happiness and a new centered, healthy beginning for Wrigley."

"You're probably getting those good readings because Zoe's outside," I joked.

Lisa rolled her eyes. "See what I mean? Ignore him."

Inviting an American Indian spiritual healer into our home with the hope of curing our sick Great Dane puppy required an open mind, but as she talked, I had to work to keep the doubts away. Warm Breeze shared her assessment that she sensed a "strong life-force and positive energy" within our home.

I didn't necessarily agree with her.

Lisa and I were depressed about Riley, the cats had been hiding out for two weeks and Wrigley was frail, could barely walk, and his coat was missing clumps of hair. Then again, I'd never seen Wrigley walk backwards, so maybe this lady did have special powers. I decided to reserve judgment. However, Wrigley's initial reaction to Warm Breeze wasn't one of open-minded healing either.

Lisa and I explained what had happened to Riley, and we provided the healer with Wrigley's medical history, starting from the day after his first vaccine shot.

She was a good listener, taking notes the entire time.

She put her notepad down and said nothing for at least a minute after we'd finished speaking.

I wasn't certain, but she might have been experiencing a mild seizure.

She waved off my concern. "I'm fine. I can't control when strong readings hit me. I'll start by telling you some things that will help you understand me and why I'm here.

"Fifteen years ago I lost my beloved Adolph, a beautiful German Shepard. He was only a puppy, nine months old. I couldn't find a vet, any specialist who could help me save my Adolph."

I'd forgotten to take my Ritalin and by now, my mind was all over. I was tired too, just about the worst combination for me. My mind wondered: Who names a German Shepard "Adolph?"

When Precious sauntered into our living room, I pondered if Warm Breeze had a cat, if its name would be Hemmler?

Every time Warm Breeze mentioned Adolph, I kicked Lisa under the coffee table. Lisa countered by driving the toe of her boot into my ankle and shifting down one cushion on the sofa.

Warm Breeze never stopped talking and didn't appear to notice the commotion.

Wrigley sighed as she spoke, his head flat on his bed. At one point he let loose a long, muffled, machine-gun sounding fart. He twitched, so I knew it was a stinker.

Warm Breeze never missed a beat, talking even as the sick smell hit us. Finally, she addressed the topic of vaccines, and I began to pay close attention.

"Bottom line is that puppies shouldn't be getting all these shots. It wreaks havoc on their immune systems. When I completed my research, I felt responsible for my poor Adolph's death. The shots, the food I gave him, all contributed to his death. That dry, store-bought dog food is full of useless and dangerous fillers, and it's killing our pets. The vets, the pharmaceutical companies and the pet food manufacturers are all in it together, motivated by money. They must be stopped."

She became more agitated as she spoke. Her voice raised and then lowered, but now her words were accompanied by wild swings of her hands and arms.

Her agitation was disconcerting. Lisa slanted me a glance without moving her head. I completely agreed with what I'm sure she was thinking. My own eyes went to Wrigley.

He wasn't lying flat anymore. His eyebrows were raised, and his face was pushed forward, but he made sure not to move any closer to us. He cocked his head left with his right ear lifted, making sure he heard everything, I'm guessing.

Finally Warm Breeze took a deep breath and said, "Forgive me. I'm very passionate."

Maybe she had finally noticed our stunned expressions.

"My passion is why I do what I do," she explained. "It's all for the animals. It's my calling."

Now that I had a chance to get in a word edgewise I cut to the chase, knowing we wouldn't be meeting with her again anytime soon.

"I'm not sure what it is you actually do? Is it a spiritual prayer or ritual?" I asked.

"It's a therapy, and with your permission I'd like to administer it to Wrigley while we're talking. I use lumen light to penetrate the affected area. After several treatments he'll be healed. I've seen it work miracles.

"The negative energy removed from Wrigley's system will leave him weak and lethargic temporarily. With each session, his sick, negative energy will be replaced with healthy, good energy. If you or Lisa have any ailments, you could benefit from the treatment as well." I thought if Wrigley became any weaker or more lethargic he'd be pronounced dead.

Lisa had been sneaking covert glances at her watch every three or four minutes. She had completely lost interest.

Against my better judgment, I asked Warm Breeze to perform the treatment on Wrigley.

She pulled what looked like a sphygmomanometer from her bag. Most people call it a blood pressure meter, but because I lived with a nurse I knew the technical name for one.

I was wrong though. The device was more like a heating pad made of a polyester-type cloth, lined with hundreds of tiny translucent beaded lights. It was the lumen light device.

Warm Breeze glided towards Wrigley with the device in her hands. He was already on full alert and quickly gauged he had only a few seconds to evade the stranger with the unknown, terrifying object in her hands.

Warm Breeze moved behind Wrigley, unknowingly placing herself where Wrigley's greatest imagined fears manifested. Because he couldn't move his neck or turn to see what was behind him, his paranoia skyrocketed, providing him a burst of energy he needed to attempt his escape.

His legs slid out. He fell, his face full of panic.

Warm Breeze proceeded like a pre-programmed robot unable or incapable of reading the most obvious signs of animal distress. She continued to arrange herself and the device.

Her unconsciousness led to Wrigley attempting a second escape, but again he fell, this time letting out a painful yelp.

I jumped off the sofa and moved to protect him.

"You need to stop. You can't just go up to him. He's particular about those kind of things," I made clear.

Warm Breeze never wavered. She was determined to give her life saving treatment to our sick puppy, even if it killed him. When she ripped off a small Velcro strip, releasing the cord to plug into the wall, Wrigley freaked out again.

I hugged him and cried out, "Please. Sit down. Let me do it. Okay?"

I turned my attention to my petrified dog. "It's alright, buddy. You're okay, Wrigley. I'm here. Nothing's going to hurt you, buddy."

After our traumatized puppy calmed down, I helped him back onto his bed.

Lisa brought over a sofa pillow so Wrigley could rest his head more comfortably.

Warm Breeze instructed me from her seat in the living room how and where to place the lumen light over Wrigley's left rear leg. After placing the light as she instructed I returned to the sofa.

Lisa stood up.

"I wish I could stay and help," she said to Warm Breeze. "I don't know if Paul told you, but I have an appointment. It was nice meeting you. Feel free to stay as long as you want." She smirked at me on her way out.

Warm Breeze didn't deter from her mission. "Wrigley's affliction is deep. He'll require several sessions. The light works on all living beings, animals and people alike. One of my clients had bad arthritis for years. She's pain free now. Of course she uses the light regularly; twice a week, for thirty minutes. Do you have any ailments, Paul?"

"I do see a chiropractor for my back," I replied.

"We'll give you a treatment when Wrigley's done," she stated.

I wanted to know what a treatment with this light cost.

I was surprised when she said "nothing."

I grew up in a family with two alcoholic parents. Innate distrust and skepticism was something I'd learned very early. My distrust of Warm Breeze decreased just the tiniest bit when she said it cost nothing.

Maybe she was a bit odd and her way different, but her heart seemed in the right place when she said, "I normally don't discuss my fee until we're done. Don't be concerned. There is no charge for my visit today. My time is my gift to you and your family, especially with your loss of Riley and what's happening with Wrigley. I look forward to the opportunity of working with you so we can bring Wrigley back to center. That's my wish and would be my greatest reward," she told me.

Wrigley snored, having fallen asleep for the first time since our guest arrived. She'd been at our house for over two hours.

I offered Warm Breeze some leftover spaghetti Lisa had made the night before Riley died.

She accepted. It was strange to be eating pasta in my living room with an American Indian spiritual healer. Wrigley had introduced all kinds of people into our life. While the light sat there being a light, we ate.

I made small talk, taking a welcome break from hearing the vast amount of information Warm Breeze had been reeling out about the things to do and not to do with Wrigley.

"Lisa and I visited Monticello last summer," I told her. "During the tour they said Virginia was home to at least sixteen known Native American tribes. Are you a descendant of one of them?"

"That's an interesting question. I'm glad you asked! After losing Adolph I went on a pilgrimage of sorts. That journey led me to what I'm doing now. During my travels out West during my soul searching exploration, I had the opportunity to meet a local chief of the Sioux nation. He is a descendant of Sitting Bull. Most people think of Sitting Bull as a great warrior, but he was first and foremost a holy and medicine man."

Warm Breeze was speaking very quietly. "The Chief told me I possessed a special gift, a gift of healing. I traced my family's ancestry.

My great grandmother's second cousin on her father's side was married to a Native American. It's a small percentage, but in my mind it qualifies me as 'Native American,' which is why for three years I've been corresponding with the Chief and the Tribal Elders.

"After the annual casino audit is certified, they promised to make a final ruling on my petition. If it all goes well, by next year, I'll officially be adopted by the Tribe." She beamed proudly at the very idea. Her story explained why she looked more Irish than Native American. I set my half empty bowl of spaghetti down and wondered what in the hell I was doing sitting here talking to this lady.

"Will we be able to see a change in Wrigley today?" I asked.

"Oh no, I think he'll need several treatments before he improves."

The timer went off. I jumped up to remove the device off Wrigley. His eyes watched every move I made, but he lay completely still. I think he may have been playing possum in the hopes we'd go back to ignoring him.

Warm Breeze was anxious to put the lumen light on my back.

"How does this work? Do you come back for every treatment, or do you leave the light with us?" I asked.

"You can purchase a lumen light from me. That's what most people prefer. We'll still meet. In fact, it's like I become part of your family." I already had enough family in my life, I thought.

"How much is it?" I asked.

"Eighteen-fifty," she said without batting an eye.

"That's incredibly reasonable if it does everything you say."

"That's what I tell people all the time, but you'd be surprised how many people don't buy it. I think it's difficult for some people to break through traditional thinking. It's people like you, Paul, that believe in the power of healing naturally and spiritually that purchase the light."

"Lisa's mom has arthritis. She could use one," I said. "We'll take two."

"Wonderful," Warm Breeze gushed. "I'm so glad Greg introduced us. You and Lisa are terrific. Wrigley's lucky to have such wonderful parents."

When she said "parents," I didn't like it. People use that term affectionately all the time concerning pets, but the way she said it made me feel queasy.

"I only have one light with me today, but I'll get you the other one tomorrow. I was planning on checking in on Wrigley anyway. I take Visa if that's easier," she said.

"No, that's fine. I used to carry a lot of cash until I got married," I said, smiling. "But I think I can cover this."

Warm Breeze's face lit up. I pulled my wallet out and placed two twenty dollar bills on the coffee table.

"You can keep the change," I said.

Warm Breeze stared at me, then started laughing. "Lisa said you were a joker. You had me going. So you want to use your credit card?"

"Thirty-seven, right? Eighteen-fifty plus eighteen-fifty is thirty-seven," I said.

Warm Breeze's face deflated. Her energy level, in my estimation, and I'm not a professional, plummeted close to Wrigley's.

"I guess I wasn't clear. It's one *thousand* eight hundred and fifty dollars for each light."

Unbelievable. It took me three hours and eating half a bowl of spaghetti to figure out what Wrigley knew three seconds after I opened the door. The spaghetti turned in my stomach. I was more disappointed than I was angry, but I had room for that and feeling taken too.

"Oh. That's a lot of money. I'll have to discuss it with Lisa first."

"Of course. I can leave this one overnight and bring the other one over tomorrow. That will give you and Lisa time to talk." She must have plugged herself into a super emotional recharger because she was animated again.

"You know, with everything we've been through, it's probably better if we don't have visitors anytime soon. Take the light with you when you go," I said.

Wrigley shifted his head up and angled his face towards the kitchen. He heard the door open.

Lisa was back.

She breezed in, probably surprised the "healer" was still here. "You guys must have had a lot to talk about. Oh, you ate? I got you a sandwich, Paul."

"Are you a runner, Lisa?" Warm Breeze interrupted. "Do you have any problems with your knees, joints?"

"No, I'm good, thanks. I'm sure we've kept you longer than you expected. Let me get my check book," Lisa said, walking towards the library.

"It's already been taken care of honey," I told her.

Warm Breeze left quickly. It may have been because she knew she'd lost a sale. Maybe she drove halfway down our street before realizing she'd been asked to leave by a lady who possessed her own mysterious and special powers. When Lisa was in her no-nonsense mood, not too many people were anxious to tangle with her.

"Maybe that tribe will change her name from Warm Breeze to Hot Air," I mused after she was finally gone.

"Dear God. When she went after Wrigley with that voodoo thing I thought he was going to kill himself trying to get away from her!" Lisa shook her head and started to giggle.

That got us both going. We laughed so hard we cried.

Abruptly, Lisa stopped laughing.

"What's wrong?" I asked.

"For a split second I forgot all about last night. You know, everything about Riley."

I hugged her and said quietly, "I know exactly how you feel."

Chapter 17

Knowing When the Help is No Longer Helpful

Lisa was pulling a fourteen-hour shift the next day at the hospital. She went to bed at seven-thirty. I turned off a repeat Seinfeld episode I'd seen at least twenty times. It was one of my favorites, but that night it was difficult to find humor in anything.

Wrigley had left his bed at least three times since Warm Breeze departed. He shared my restlessness.

I caught him out of his bed lurking several times. He wandered around the kitchen, first looking down the stairwell to the basement, and then he'd go check the stairs going up to the bedrooms.

Five minutes outside to complete his business extended to ten and fifteen minute periods without him doing anything but sniffing. That's when it hit me. Wrigley was exhausting what little energy he had left in hopes of tracking a fresh scent of his lost companion, Riley.

Stretching his neck as high as he could manage, he forced his big black nose into the air, hunting in every direction. He desperately sought out his missing friend. By the end of the day, completely spent, I think he knew his efforts were futile. He would never be with Riley again.

The next morning, Wrigley didn't eat or drink.

The cats appeared after hearing the snap of the lid being pulled off their canned food. The food stank, but they came running. All three meowed, dancing between my legs and brushing against me in harmony, waiting for their morning fix of Fancy Feast. The food orgy happened once in the evening too. Currently it was the best way to keep track of them because they had been keeping low profiles. Maybe they feared they would be next to disappear, knowing Riley was gone and Wrigley was close to it.

I dished out nearly equal portions to each cat. Precious received an extra spoonful because he looked bigger with his puffy Himalayan hair.

I popped open a fourth can, confusing all three cats.

Ignoring their hopeful glances, I put the food on a dessert plate, took it into the dining room and placed it in front of Wrigley's face. He sniffed it, twitching his nose like a rabbit. I placed the plate directly in front of his mouth.

His large tongue made a cameo appearance, lapping half the food into his mouth with one swipe and dropping the remaining food onto his bed. I scooped up what was left of the disgusting mush and let him eat the rest off my hand.

"You might live another day, Wrigley," I said solemnly. I tried to conceal my grief, knowing he shared it, possibly even more then I could appreciate.

With Riley gone, Wrigley spiraled to a new low. During the day when I took Wrigley out, it became necessary for me to use a bath towel wrapped around his belly, which I pulled up on, allowing him to stand and pee. He hadn't pooped in two days. That wasn't surprising because the cat food he'd eaten was the biggest meal, if you could call it that, he'd consumed in the last forty-eight hours.

I tried reading to take my mind off Wrigley. I had to reread the Washington Post article about the fees on the Dulles Toll Road. I had to read it three times to remember how much and when the increase was occurring. I swore that road paid for the entire state's budget.

I finally put the paper aside and leafed through the literature Warm Breeze had left us. She'd mentioned a holistic vet, a Dr. McIntyre, who worked with large animals, such as horses and other livestock. Wrigley was a mini-horse in my mind.

I read on the internet that Dr. McIntyre also practiced acupuncture and used herbal therapies to help animals recover.

I'd left a message at the orthopedic specialist's office begging them to move up Wrigley's appointment. I'd offered to fill in for any cancellation, but nobody called back.

I was confident Wrigley wasn't going to make it another five days.

When I called Dr. Shiller he suggested keeping Wrigley comfortable by increasing his pain medication to the maximum dosage, three Tylenol codeine-based pain pills each day. Two pills already put Wrigley in a near catatonic state. Three pills might very well have served as a passive act of euthanasia. I couldn't do it, but I thought about it more than once.

My crew supervisor called me that afternoon informing me he needed a new heat gun to expedite a drywall repair and a taller extension ladder to reach the top of a chimney. He also informed me that Jose had not shown up for work for the last two days.

I didn't care. I authorized him to buy whatever he needed to get the project done. I needed additional money coming in because of the dogs, but instead of doing something to make that happen, I was taking the opposite road and ignoring my responsibilities. After the crew supervisor hung up, I found myself staring at Dr. McIntyre's card on our coffee table.

What the hell did I have to lose? Maybe I should call the holistic vet as a last resort for getting Wrigley some help. I couldn't concentrate on anything else, even though I'd taken my Ritalin. Because of my training and the work I'd done with support groups I recognized what was happening, but I couldn't do anything to change it. My mind and heart were not always in concert. When I facilitated grief groups people often shared how difficult it was to concentrate after they'd lost someone. I took Prozac for six months after my mom died. I also stopped working at hospice. I didn't have the energy to help others with their grief.

Lisa was a saint for putting up with my mood swings and depression back then. I think going to work may have been a blessing for her while I was grieving. When people asked me why I stopped doing bereavement work, I joked it off. "It's a dead-end job," I'd say, but the truth was that it was too painful after losing my mom.

Once my grief became less debilitating, I had a more profound awareness of how deeply I respected and appreciated Lisa. Her tolerance and the love she offered me when I didn't have much to offer her in return was a testament to who she was and is. I'd be the first to admit I was difficult to live with, especially during that time. I loved her all the more for hanging in there with me. Lisa was a fighter, and she didn't quit or surrender easily, if ever. Sometimes people only realize things like that after someone's gone. I was a fortunate man to know it and to still have her with me.

Chapter 18

Small Wonder

As I sat there thinking about how much joy Wrigley had given me and some of the steps I'd taken to get where I was today, I made up my mind. I called Dr. McIntyre.

I listened to the voice recording of Dr. McIntyre's machine three times before sorting the days and times she was available. I finally called the clinic twenty minutes before they opened that afternoon, hoping to speak to someone who could help me get Wrigley in to see the holistic vet immediately.

"Dr. McIntyre only works out of this office twice a week. Her appointments take place mostly in the field. I'm sorry Mr. Sullivan, she's booked solid until early May," the receptionist, Frankie, told me.

My dad was a professional salesman, just like his father. He loved "the game," the excitement and rush of making a sale. It was his "crack cocaine." His addiction cost him two wives and the opportunity to understand the gratification of being a father. I was a good salesman, but I'd gone in a different direction, earning an MSW in social work school rather than an MBA. My father's dream of me carrying on the "Sullivan selling torch" went out before it was little more than a spark. Although, being Dad, he never quit trying to sell me on the idea.

I'd learned things good and bad from my dad. After years of watching him sell and being on the other end of it at times, I knew how it was done. I wasn't above using his old school techniques, especially given my current situation. To obtain even a small comfort for Wrigley and ease my own pain and guilt for considering putting him down, my pleading to Frankie was a mastery of manipulation. I rationalized it because it was all true. But it was how I delivered the truth that made me ask, was I any different than my father? At the moment, seeking help for Wrigley, I didn't care.

"Three days ago my wife and I lost our eight-month-old Great Dane puppy, Riley. I'm calling about her half-brother, Wrigley. He's seriously ill, probably dying. He needs Dr. McIntyre's help. He won't make it until May or even to next week without some kind of intervention. I can't watch my wife lose another puppy. We don't have kids. It's a long story, but if there's anything you can do, anything, I'm begging you, please help us."

"Be quiet, completely silent after asking for the sale," my dad would tell me. "Whoever speaks first, Paul, loses."

I shut up, waiting for an answer from the kind receptionist. There was nothing but silence from the phone for five or six seconds, which felt like a long time. I didn't speak.

"Mr. Sullivan, I'll give you a call back. I'm not promising you anything. Let me see if there's something I can do," Frankie finally said.

When the vet's receptionist told me she'd call back, I knew Wrigley had an appointment. My dad sold expensive medical equipment. To close a deal he had to obtain an appointment with the doctor first.

"The most important person who determines whether you get the sale is the person setting up appointments," my dad taught me. "Half the time that is the person running the office. The receptionist, the person answering the phones, controls who gets through the door." Ten minutes later Frankie called me back. "Eight o'clock tomorrow morning. Dr. McIntyre is coming in early for Wrigley, so please don't be late. Her schedule is completely full. I can't allow her to fall behind."

I understood the rush my dad sought during his life of selling. For me, the short-lived adrenalin rush wasn't worth the effort and collateral damage he caused achieving it, but in this case, I was grateful for his training.

"Thank you. You have no idea what a relief this is. Please tell Dr. McIntyre thank you as well. We'll be there early, I promise. Thank you, Frankie. You're awesome."

Precious jumped up on my chair, wanting some attention after the call ended. "Meeeoow." He rubbed his head against my arms.

I gave him a quick petting. "Sorry, buddy. I know you're getting robbed, but you're going to have to hang in there for just a while longer." In a never-ending hurry, I set him down on the floor, leaving him standing alone in the room, meowing for more attention.

Riley had died Monday night. The "healer" came Tuesday afternoon. Wednesday, what remained of Wrigley's puppy personality and spirit evaporated. On Thursday, by seven forty-five in the morning, Lisa was busy at work and her mom was packing in South Carolina, preparing for her five day stay with us. She was to arrive Friday.

I was at Dr. McIntyre's office waiting. The office was located in a historic home, built in the late 1800s, in the quaint little town of Clifton, Virginia.

Wrigley was sleeping in the back of the SUV when a train whistle blew as it crossed the tracks through the middle of town. The sound took me back to visiting my grandmother in Riverside, Illinois, as a kid. We'd walk together to the train depot three blocks from her home. We'd then set a penny on the railroad track and wait for the locomotive to press Lincoln's face into a cartoon character.

One time, picking up the coin too early, I discovered how hot it was. I dropped the coin, losing it under the track, and was unable to retrieve it. I bawled, wishing I had another penny for the next passing train.

"I don't have another penny honey," my grandmother told me. "But I have a nickel."

She unclasped her change pocket from her clutch. My oblong, fat-faced Thomas Jefferson, quarter-sized nickel was the prize piece in my funny-money collection.

I spent a weekend alone with my Grandma and Aunt Marie, once a year, without any of my siblings. Those were the best weeks of my childhood. I wondered what I'd be like today if I'd ever felt the special attention and love from my parents the way I did from my grandmother.

Just before eight an elderly lady, maybe five-foot-one, climbed out of a mid-sized Lexus SUV. She had parked in the spot posted with a sign reading, "No Parking."

I nodded a greeting as she passed me. She waved at me to follow her, pointing at the little house.

The gravel lot bothered Wrigley's paws, so I picked him up and carried him into the clinic. Frankie, the receptionist, held the old wooden screen door open for me.

"Do you carry him everywhere?" The little old lady's voice broke into my concentration as I set Wrigley down.

Startled, I jumped. "Whoa, you scared me!"

"That's a first, huh, Frankie? Tiny little me scaring a big, strong man." She smiled and turned toward me, allowing me to see the embroidered name on the left breast pocket of her white coat, "Dr. McIntyre, DVM."

"Based on your entrance, I am guessing he doesn't do stairs?" she asked politely.

"Not for the last month. He did before getting really sick. Even then he'd start but stop about halfway. Wrigley never has things easy," I replied.

"He's a big dog for you to be carrying around all the time."

"Yeah, but it's easier because in unfamiliar places, he panics."

Dr. McIntyre opened a door adjacent to the small waiting area. "Have him come in here. I want to see him walk, if he can," she said, leading the way.

I always led and Wrigley followed. It was something I'd learned watching "The Dog Whisperer." I sure was one hell of a pack leader, with one puppy dead and one dying.

Wrigley eased forward, but stopped after each step, unfamiliar with the creaking sound of the oak-planked floor.

Dr. McIntyre knelt down in the center of the room next to two thick bath mats.

"Can you come over here, handsome fellow?" she cajoled.

"If you don't mind, I'd rather sit over here," I almost said. It was the first time my mind snapped with humor since losing Riley. Humor was, of course, my way of relieving nervousness or anxiety.

Surprisingly, Wrigley answered her request, plopping down exactly where she pointed on the center of the rugs.

Dr. McIntyre's examination began exactly the way Dr. Blabey's had started.

She didn't, however, ask me whether Wrigley was friendly. She got right down to business. I sat in a large rocking chair in the corner of the room, rocking slowly back and forth.

"Help me turn him over, onto his other side," she said, before I could get too relaxed. "Horses do the same thing when they're injured." Dr. McIntyre showed me how Wrigley was protecting his hurt leg. "Animals, like people, need to trust. I never start manipulating their bodies or go to the problem area first. You have to build trust first."

The vet was tiny and seemed more so when she leaned over Wrigley. How did someone her age and size manipulate animals as big as a horse? I peeked at the date on her Doctorate diploma. I think it said she graduated in 1963, the year I was born. Holy cow! Impressive. The diploma reminded me that my birthday was tomorrow, but I wasn't the least bit excited about it.

"He's not going to stand for me so you'll need to lift him up," she said.

I interlocked my hands under Wrigley's belly, lifting his back end off the ground. I'd done this many times during his examinations. It was the primary cause of my back pain.

Wrigley managed to muster enough energy to walk forward, leaving me with the choice of following him in a hunched man parody or dropping him, defeating the purpose of holding him up.

I wondered if Wrigley secretly possessed a wicked sense of humor with me the "butt" of his jokes. Knowing the room ended in ten feet, I hobbled along with him, trashing my back some more.

"That's fine," Dr. McIntyre said. "Hold him steady." His position may have been fine for her and Wrigley, but I was leaning over, pulling up on a ninety-pound, deadweight dog, with the pain in my back growing exponentially. I was about to drop him when Dr. McIntyre said, "Perfect, keep him in that position."

My face was inches from Wrigley's butt and a foot from Dr. McIntyre's face. For a change, I ended up farting. For the love of farting dogs everywhere, did I have to suffer *every* embarrassment possible? I quickly blamed Wrigley, but I'm sure the vet was on to me.

She stretched Wrigley's bad leg despite the fog I had just provided. From my point of view, it looked like she was going to snap his leg off, like breaking the coveted Thanksgiving turkey wishbone.

When Wrigley's left rear paw passed the height of his left ear, he turned his head sharply, showing his teeth to Dr. McIntyre.

She immediately released his leg. "You can set him down now."

I felt like I had just finished the second of three of my old high school wrestling matches. After holding Wrigley's body in a hovering position for over six minutes without a break, I wasn't sure if I won or lost the match. Sweat poured down my forehead and rolled down my arms and off my hands.

I collapsed back onto the rocker, knocking into the wall with the back of my head. I pretended it didn't hurt and grabbed some Kleenex to wipe off my face. I wasn't sure if the pain caused me to sweat from my eyes or if I was actually crying.

Dr. McIntyre began chiropractic exercises on Wrigley's spine and legs. She treated his hurt leg last. When she finished she said, "I wish chiropractic manipulation or acupuncture could help him, but I don't think it will. He's got a serious problem, and it's not an orthopedic issue. I believe he's in the middle of a neurological emergency. While what I did today will help ease some pain, I believe he's in the first stages of paralysis, and may lose his ability to walk permanently."

I wasn't completely surprised, but it was still shocking to hear. My mom was in a coma for almost a week with instructions not to take measures to extend her life. Yet, when the call came, "Mom's gone," it was a jarring surprise. It made no sense to be surprised, but the finality of hearing she was really dead still had carried the power to shock me.

Obviously, we knew something serious was happening with Wrigley, but hearing it moved the situation to a different level.

"What do you mean by neurological?" I asked.

"His lameness is a result of something taking place much higher up his spine. The first thing I noticed when he walked in was how he keeps his head down and face forward. His range of motion is restricted. His head stays down because he can't lift it any higher without pain.

"I'm sure you thought I was going to break his leg when I pulled it as far as I did. No animal would've allowed me to do that if it was an orthopedic issue. No matter how I pulled it, up, out, back or forth, he didn't respond until I reached that extreme point. There's no doubt in my mind this is neurological, and it's serious."

Frankie knocked at the door. "Dr. McIntyre?"

"I'm just wrapping up. Give me two minutes," she responded.

I looked at the clock on the wall. It was nine-fifteen. She'd spent an hour and fifteen minutes with Wrigley. There was a commotion in the tiny waiting area behind the door as it filled with several people and their pets.

"Toxins are released after a treatment, especially after the first one," Dr. McIntyre said, removing her hands from Wrigley and standing. "He's going to be more exhausted than usual after this. I'm going to be blunt. Wrigley's at a critical point. Time is an issue here."

She handed me a business card. "I have great confidence in this neurologist. He's going to want an MRI done on Wrigley. If you don't do something immediately, he will lose the use of his other leg. If you decide to go forward with the surgery, let me know. Acupuncture is excellent for managing pain, and I can help him with that once his other issues are fixed. Good luck."

Wrigley had fallen asleep and showed no signs of wanting to get up.

"Help me move this chair." Dr. McIntyre pointed to the rocker where I was sitting and banging my head.

She pulled hard at a stuck door that led outside. "Frankie will mail you an invoice. Go out this way, and you'll avoid the chaos that awaits me." Her smile was kind, but there was sadness and sympathy radiating from her because of Wrigley's dire condition.

"Thank you so much for seeing us. I appreciate the special appointment. I haven't seen Wrigley this relaxed in weeks. Thank you."

Dr. McIntyre had told me Wrigley would be exhausted, but forgot to warn me he'd be explosive too. He farted the entire way home. Maybe it was payback for blaming him in the doctor's office. Still, I noticed an improvement in the way he walked into the house. I wasn't naive enough to believe it was going to last, but it was something.

"Critical point," was the exact wording I'd heard four days earlier, but it was for Riley that time. Normally, I would have called Lisa to fill her in on the latest, but this time I didn't. We'd talk when she got home in the evening. She didn't need to hear the bad news with ten more hours of nursing in front of her and an hour long drive home.

* * *

That night Lisa and I discussed canceling her mother's visit, but decided against it. With Lisa off the next five days, I was looking forward to having my dog responsibilities split with her. It was an understatement to say I was burned out with doggy duties.

Before going to sleep, I went downstairs and laid next to Wrigley with my head next to his. His big brown eyes oozed with discharge. He looked at me sideways and let out a long sigh when I placed my hand gently on his head.

"My four-legged Humpty Dumpty. How is it you're still standing?" I whispered.

Friday morning Lisa left to pick up her mom. The neurosurgeon Dr. McIntyre referred personally called me back just after Lisa left for the airport.

"Mike Knoeckel, returning your call. I spoke with Dr. McIntyre this morning about Wrigley. Can you bring him in this morning at eleven forty-five?" he asked.

"Absolutely." I couldn't believe we'd waited over three weeks to see an orthopedist, and Dr. McIntyre managed Wrigley an appointment with a neurologist in less than twenty-four hours. We owed her.

Lisa was taking her mom to lunch and shopping. Dr. Knoeckel worked at South Paws, the animal hospital where Riley had died four days earlier. Lisa wouldn't want to go back there, and I hadn't been able to tell her Dr. McIntyre's diagnosis and prognosis for Wrigley the previous evening because she was exhausted when she got home from work. That was the reason I had held off telling her the sobering news.

Wrigley and I walked into South Paws Animal Hospital ten minutes early. It may have been my imagination, but it seemed everyone watched Wrigley slump and swagger slowly through the main door and up to the receptionist. At barely ten months, he looked like an old, dying dog. In fact, I'm sure some people believed I was there to put him down. Any relief Dr. McIntyre had given him was gone. He could barely walk, and I could barely pick him up because my back was in miserable shape. We were quite the pair.

I waited in a consultation room next to the room where we had lost Riley. Wrigley turned around four times before he dropped down on the carpet in the center of the room. There was a light tap at the door, and a tall, fit man in Wrangler blue jeans and cowboy boots walked into the room.

"Michael Knoeckel," he said, before moving directly to the floor next to Wrigley.

"Stay where you are big boy," he told Wrigley, placing his hands on his body to keep him from getting up.

He asked when Wrigley's leg first went lame and how long his neck had been immobile. I watched as the surgeon pulled and pushed Wrigley's limbs much like the other doctors had done. Dr. Knoeckel extended Wrigley's left rear leg further than anyone had before.

Wrigley submitted to the prodding until then, but as the leg extended, he growled and showed his teeth. The growl was faint, but his message was clear.

"Dr. McIntyre's diagnosis is correct. I'm glad she called me. This is an emergency situation. His knee may be an orthopedic issue, but it's also connected to a neurological problem. We can't know what's happening with this boy until he has an MRI. They are not cheap. If you can get there by two, I can get you scheduled today," he said.

I couldn't make the decision without talking to Lisa. Her mom's flight had been held up in Charlotte, and she was still waiting at the airport when I called her.

She didn't say a word as I relayed what Dr. McIntyre said the day before, followed by Dr. Knoeckel's recommendation. The MRI would cost $2200. Surgery would be at least double that.

Lisa didn't hesitate.

"We have to know what's wrong with him before we make any decisions. Let's go ahead with the MRI," she said.

Before she hung up she said, "Make sure you don't use the American Express card. That has all of Riley's charges on it. Use the Visa. Thanks for doing this. Hey, let's not tell Mom anything. I haven't told her about Riley yet. It'll be too much for her."

The money had always been a concern, but now it was becoming a real problem. On Monday, Dr. Shiller's fee was $450. The emergency hospital charged us $1368.00.

Lisa had wanted Riley cremated separately from other animals and a fancy wooden box for her ashes, so that added an additional $200.00 to the fee. We'd spent $2233.00 in the past week, and five times that on Wrigley's care since he entered our lives.

Lisa's mom had never met Wrigley or Riley other than through our stories, pictures and one video. The video of the puppies playing tug-of-war on the side of the house was recorded a month after Riley came into our lives, just after Christmas, when everything was so perfect.

The MRI Imaging Center was located in Vienna, twenty minutes from South Paws Hospital. I arrived ten minutes before two and Wrigley was taken back immediately.

I waited for an hour and a half before being called back to see Wrigley in the recovery room.

The African-American lady who led me back to see him was about sixty years old. She was kind and had a sweet, innocent, childlike voice, despite her years. "I thought you'd want to be with him when he wakes up," she said.

Wrigley lay on his left side on a large table covered with white sheets and a soft blanket. His tongue hung from his mouth. It was dry, pinkish and lifeless.

"Is that normal?" I asked.

"Sure it is. You'll know he's coming out of it when he pulls his tongue back in."

I blinked. "It's wigging me out. Can you put it back in his mouth? Is it dangerous?"

"Men and dogs. I swear, the bigger you are, the more squeamish you are." She laughed at me, splashed water on Wrigley's tongue and scooted it back into his mouth.

When my mom was dying her lips were dry, especially towards the end. Lisa showed me how to roll a damp cotton swab over my mother's lips to moisten them. Seeing Wrigley's tongue out reminded me of her discomfort, and I didn't want to see it.

A bit later, another attendant asked, "Did Sherri bring you back here?"

"Yes."

"She knows better than that. People freak out seeing their pets like this. Sherri's got a soft spot for folks she thinks need special time with their pet. Don't worry, you can stay. Look, he's coming out of it now. See his eyes moving?" The man then walked out without waiting for an answer.

Evidently getting Wrigley to lie still for the MRI was as challenging as trying to weigh him. It required three technicians and extra medication despite Wrigley's weak condition. He could put up a fight when he felt it necessary.

I pulled the SUV to the rear of the building. Two gentlemen in blue scrubs hoisted Wrigley from a table on wheels into the back of the Yukon.

"Damn, I could sleep pretty good back here," the one guy said, pushing his hand down onto Wrigley's plush, soft comforter blanketing his dog bed.

Wrigley was groggy, but appeared to know he was going home because he lifted his head up and sighed when I kissed his forehead. His breath was horrendous. In the big picture, it was a small thing to contend with considering everything I'd just found out.

Sherri, the lady who'd taken me back during his recovery, came out to say goodbye. "Nobody spends the money you just did for an animal they don't love. I've learned a lot and seen a lot of things while working here. When things are difficult to accept, I put my trust in God." She nodded sagely.

I closed the rear hatch, moved to the driver's seat and said goodbye. Sherri waved to me and signaled me to roll down my window. I did and she called out, "I'm praying for him. And I'll pray for you too."

As I drove away, I wondered if God involved himself in such matters. Either way, I accepted her blessing and hoped He was listening.

Chapter 19

Paralyzing Decision

I was relieved not seeing Lisa's car in the driveway when I returned home with Wrigley. She and her mom must have extended their shopping spree. I was glad she was doing something she enjoyed. Lately, I'd forgotten how that felt.

I set Wrigley on the lawn to pee and waited, but he plopped down on the grass instead of taking care of his business.

When I set him back down inside the house, my shirt sleeves had dog crap on them. Poor pooch must have laid in his own poop. The smell was suffocating. I wasn't even put out by it, just sad, mostly for him. He was a proud animal. I knew he couldn't have felt good not being able to care for himself. I wiped the crap off him. I threw my soiled shirt in the trash.

He was in such bad shape, I wondered if he'd survive until we got the MRI results on Monday. The desperate theme was becoming all too familiar and frankly, I hated it.

I picked up the Post, looked at the date and remembered it was my birthday. I hoped Lisa and her mom weren't planning to surprise me with anything. I didn't want to go out for dinner either. My idea of a big celebration for my forty-fifth birthday was to not have to take Wrigley out for his last pee and to be in bed asleep by nine.

In hindsight, we should have asked Lisa's mom to postpone her visit. Lisa and I needed time together. We hadn't had a free moment to process what had happened on Monday with Riley. And we still had to decide what we were going to do about Wrigley.

Would we try to save him? Was it even possible? Or would we be forced to let him go, like Riley? The idea of losing both our puppies in less than two weeks was incomprehensible, but it was a real possibility.

My two hours alone in the house before Lisa and her mom returned was a welcome respite. I napped on Wrigley's sofa with Precious sleeping on the cushion above my head and Cassie curled up next to my chest. Wrigley lay on his bed and slept the entire time too.

Lisa's surprise for my birthday was that she didn't bake a cake, get me a gift or a birthday card. I didn't care because I understood having no energy or desire to celebrate anything less than a miracle for Wrigley.

"I'm sorry the celebration is so small, Paul," Lisa said after dinner. "But I didn't completely forget you."

She and her mom stepped out of the dining room and returned with three cupcakes, one with a lit birthday candle. "Guess which one is yours," Mama Hegler asked, pointing to the only one with the small candle and tiny flame.

They sang Happy Birthday. I blew out my candle and ate my cupcake in three bites.

"I'm tired. I'm going to eat this in my room and watch a movie," Mama Hegler announced. Before she went up she confided in me, "Honey, everyone has a birthday like this in their life. The trick is to avoid another one like it. I believe things will work out for Wrigley. I just have a feeling. Goodnight." She gently touched my hand before going up the stairs.

Sunday, I gave Wrigley three pills of the Tylenol with codeine. He slept for ten hours straight. He'd eaten half a bowl of dry food in four days. I gave him water via a syringe, trying to keep him from completely dehydrating.

He smelled bad. The cats stayed far away and the odor made me want to keep my distance too, but I didn't and neither did Lisa.

Lisa's mom spent most of her time that weekend in the guest bedroom, watching TV and talking to her sister and best friend, JoAnn, on the phone. It wasn't a very fun trip for her, but our exhaustion left us with little to offer. We didn't need to take Wrigley with us to discuss our options with Dr. Knoeckel. We'd already agreed to hold off making any decision on the spot. We wanted time to absorb the information regarding Wrigley's prognosis and possible treatment options, if there were any.

Lisa hesitated when we walked into the lobby of South Paws, the loss of Riley a week ago etched across her face.

We waited only a few minutes before a young attendant called us back to the same little conference room, in the back corner of the waiting area, where we had said goodbye to Riley.

"You okay with this?" I asked Lisa. "I bet she could put us in another room if we explained."

"I'll be fine." She took a deep breath as if she was about to dive into deep water.

We both stared at the center of the carpet where we had spent our last time with Riley. I broke the silence after a minute or two.

"Maybe we're unknowingly the main characters in a modern Greek tragedy," I mused.

"Hopefully it has a happy ending, if we are," Lisa responded.

"Always an optimist, aren't you? I think the optimal word in those things is 'tragedy.' I'm not sure, but I don't recall any with a happy ending."

Lisa pulled a Kleenex from a square box. Almost half the tissues came out.

She took two, wiped her nose and put the rest in her purse. "I still can't believe she's gone." Tears started to bubble. We could hear lots of activity on the other side of the door; the animal hospital was doing a brisk business this Monday morning.

As sad as it was, I was glad they put us in this particular room. It was a sacred place and provided a peaceful isolation from the outside activity.

Finally, there was a knock on the door. It opened slowly. Dr. Knoeckel could sense or see the grief on our faces because his face fell as he entered the room.

"I'm Mike Knoeckel," he said, extending his hand to Lisa and nodding recognition to me. "I want to say how sorry I am about Riley. I just found out she was your puppy. You two have had a tough time of it lately. Being here can't be fun."

We gave weak murmured responses.

"Was Riley blood-related to Wrigley?" he asked.

Lisa left me to answer. "Same father, different mothers. They were born two weeks apart," I said.

"The staff, especially Dr. Gerhardt, was profoundly touched by your loss. Everyone working that night was affected. I'm sorry I didn't recognize how difficult it must have been for you to meet with me on

Friday, Paul. I wish I'd known. I'm very sorry and unfortunately, I'm afraid what we're going to discuss today is only going to add to your pain."

We nodded, and he continued.

"I reviewed the MRI with our orthopedic surgeon this morning. Wrigley has marked proliferation of the right facet region, C2 and C3, with moderate enhancement. That's causing dramatic cord compression at the site. That's the precipitating cause of his lameness in his left rear quadrant. There may be a separate orthopedic issue there as well, which may complicate or coincide with the diagnosis and any possible treatment. Wrigley's thrown us several variables and unknowns. Unfortunately, the MRI isn't definitive," he said.

"Is it something surgery can correct?" Lisa asked.

I had no idea what Dr. Knoeckel had just told us. I heard cord compression that was causing the lameness. The rest was foreign to me.

"Correct what? I'm not clear on what you just explained," I said.

Dr. Knoeckel picked up a small model of a canine's spine and placed two fingers on two vertebra behind the neck.

"Wrigley's number 2 and 3 cervical vertebrae are being compressed under great pressure, all of the time. We don't know what is causing the compression. To answer your question Lisa, surgical decompression could be curative if it's a benign hypertrophy. If it's a neoplastic process, we would expect regrowth and likely recurrence of these signs. If this is an osteochondroma, regrowth should stop, but only as Wrigley stops growing. He's young, still developing, making it uncertain how much cord compression may recur, if any, in that time," he explained further.

"What about medication?" I asked.

"Wrigley's continuing to lose mobility in his hind quarters. He's well on his way to paralysis. Doing nothing guarantees he will become permanently paralyzed. He's already dragging his left leg. That stiffness will increase until he's too wobbly and unstable to walk. Eventually he won't be able to stand at all. At that point, he'll never walk again. Medications will only mask the inevitable, but it won't slow it down. His nerves will die and once they're dead, they can't rejuvenate. We won't know how much of his current debilitation is caused by compression or nerve damage unless we perform surgery. He's almost at a point where pain medication won't mask his pain. He's in critical condition and possibly has already passed a point of no return."

I looked at Lisa. She looked at me. We looked at Dr. Knoeckel, but neither of us said anything. It was too much information and all bad.

"I'm sure making a decision about Wrigley now must be unimaginably difficult so close to losing Riley. There are plenty of unknowns here, and his prognosis isn't good. If you elect to go forward with surgery, that itself is risky. He could become paralyzed on the table," he warned us.

He kept talking and everything he said made sense, but it didn't make anything easier.

"I wouldn't do the surgery if I believed there was no chance of recovery but to be clear, the odds aren't in Wrigley's favor. I don't wish to sound crude or unsympathetic, and I wish I could offer you more time to decide, but I can't. It's crucial you make a decision within a week and that's pushing it out. I perform surgeries on Tuesdays and Thursdays. We can schedule him for next week if you decide to go ahead. I've said a lot, and I'm sure you'll have questions for me. Do you have any now?"

I had a thousand questions but asked none because I was completely overwhelmed.

"In your assessment, what level of pain is Wrigley experiencing?" Lisa asked.

"I'd put him at a nine or ten. He won't be ambulatory much longer. We can give him some stronger pain medication. He'll sleep most of the time, but it will keep him calm." He waited another beat, we said nothing and he left us alone in the room.

Lisa and I remained sitting for several minutes without talking until I stood up. "Let's get the hell out of here," I said, reaching for her hand.

Before we made it to the exit doors of the lobby, Dr. Knoeckel called out to us.

"Take this," he said, extending his business card. "I've written my cell phone on the back. Call me anytime if you have any questions, even if it's about something we already discussed. If you do want to go forward and there's a scheduling problem, call me."

I remember walking outside. Brilliant sunshine and warm air heralded spring. Lisa and I had plans for a garden in the backyard of our new home, but no dirt would be moved that day.

The beautiful weather mocked us, adding to my sense of bad luck. Repeating the heartbreaking decision to end our puppy's life, again, was unimaginable and probable at the same time. It was too much, too soon.

On the way home, Lisa broke the silence. "I liked Dr. Knoeckel. He reminds me of a surgeon at my hospital. I do think he can save Wrigley."

I didn't respond. What could I say? I didn't like him and I didn't think there was a chance in hell he could save Wrigley? I knew where she stood on the issue. I admired her clarity and hope. I was equally clear with my stressed-out feelings and yearning for relief.

After pulling into our driveway, I accidentally put the Yukon in reverse, instead of park.

We rolled back toward the street. "Shit. I'm driving like our lives, backwards." I slapped the steering wheel with my right hand, "This sucks, Lisa. It fucking sucks."

That Monday night I had no problem being the only person pouring wine from the second bottle. The drugs we had to give Wrigley nearly knocked him unconscious. He required strong encouragement to wake up to go out.

I set him under the Japanese Snowbell tree on the front lawn. He didn't sniff, move or pee.

"Show me something, big boy. I know you're a proud Great Dane puppy, but I know you have limits, too. You don't deserve any more pain, buddy." I buried my head into his bony ribcage and began bawling like a baby.

"Lisa, come up here, please," her mom called out from the upstairs guest bedroom.

Lisa spent some time explaining to her mother what was going on. She knew we needed time and space alone.

Lisa told me later that her mother completely believed I would save Wrigley.

We took her mom to the airport early Tuesday morning. I was relieved to know she was on her way home.

Lisa went grocery shopping after we returned from the airport.

While she was gone I called Wrigley's primary vet, Dr. Shiller. We had discussed, once before, end-of-life for pets. His belief was animals shouldn't struggle or live in pain for any extended period of time. Wrigley's quality of life had been compromised, not to mention my own, and I wanted his input.

"You've read Dr. Knoeckel's report and prognosis?" I asked him. "I know you won't tell me what we should do, but I wanted to hear your insight."

"If he were five or six years old, I'd say don't even try it. But Wrigley's proven he's resilient. Puppies bounce back from bad things and recover much faster than older dogs. The odds are against him, but Wrigley is loved. Don't underestimate that. It often evens out the odds." He paused and then said, "I'd say give the surgery a chance."

After hanging up, I realized I had wanted to hear a different answer. I pulled Dr. Knoeckel's card from my wallet, calling the number he'd written on the back. I asked him the same basic question.

"Wrigley's prognosis is bleak. That still holds," Dr. Knoeckel repeated. "That said, I wouldn't attempt surgery if I didn't believe Wrigley had a chance of recovering. There are too many variables for me to be optimistic, but I'm not fatalistic, either," he told me.

Tuesday afternoon Lisa and I sat on Wrigley's sofa in the living room. All three cats lay around us, demanding some attention. Lisa delivered her final plea, hoping I'd see things her way and try to save Wrigley.

"I understand the money issue, Paul. But we can use the zero percent interest Visa, and I'll work extra hours at the hospital to help pay it off. I know the procedure's risky, but I've watched surgeons at the hospital. The last thing they want is to lose a patient. They don't volunteer to fail. I can see it in Dr. Knoeckel's face; he believes he can save Wrigley. I'm telling you, Paul, I can feel it in my heart." Like a perfect salesman, she delivered her pitch and then didn't say another word.

She was probably disappointed that my only response was, "It's been six hours. I need to wake Wrigley up to see if he'll pee."

Wrigley squirmed as I lifted him off his bed. The increased medication must have been keeping the pain at bay because he got up and walked outside on his own.

It took him several minutes to get from the dining room to his favorite pee spot, but he made it. The branches of the boxwood, one step off the breezeway, were dead from his soakings. Wrigley humped his back to poop.

I walked through the breezeway into the garage to get a doggy poop bag. I'd only pulled off four bags in the last seven days. When I returned out front, a stranger stood over Wrigley, holding his tags, trying to read them.

"What can I do for you?" I asked.

"This your dog?" the stranger asked me.

"He is. Why do you want to know?"

"I was driving by. Saw him standing out here alone. He was falling over. I was checking his collar. I thought he might be a stray," he explained.

"He's ours," I said. I might have been a tad defensive.

"I'm sorry. I didn't mean any harm," the man said.

I turned my back on him, tugged at Wrigley's collar lightly, and we headed back into the house.

I had been completely rude to the guy. He had been concerned, and I treated him like a criminal. I wished I had behaved differently, but he was gone. Using my anger and dismissing someone like they were trash was a futile way to grasp for control.

"Damn Wrigley, that dude thought you were a stray." I thought about how a month earlier people stopped in front of our house to meet Wrigley and Riley, not to check tags in case animal control was needed. At that moment I made up my mind. It was the first time I'd felt at peace since Riley died.

Lisa was crying when we walked back in. I didn't tell her what happened. She started talking before I could.

"I know the majority of Wrigley's care lands on you, and I understand it's a burden. I'm willing to accept whatever decision you make, but I want you to promise me something if you decide you don't want to go forward with his surgery. I want the space and the time to be sad as long as I need. Please don't take that away from me too," she sniffled.

"You know, you're beautiful when you're fighting for Wrigley. I can't imagine looking into your eyes knowing I was the reason he isn't a part of us, especially after losing Riley. Let's give our pathetic, proud Great Dane puppy one last chance. Let's do it," I said.

She jumped up and nearly buried me in a hug. "Mom said you'd come around. How does she know you so well?"

I'd missed her beaming smile and bright blue eyes shining with excitement. I knew we'd made the best decision for us; no matter the outcome.

Lisa grabbed my hand. "Let's tell Wrigley together!"

Chapter 20

Praying for a Miracle

The scheduler of surgeries had left for the day by the time we called. Lisa called Dr. Knoeckel on his cell phone. Maybe she was worried I would change my mind.

"Let's plan on Thursday for the surgery. Nothing to eat for him after two AM, but water is fine. Stop all his medication by nine AM. Bring him in at one-thirty. See you then." Dr. Knoeckel was professional, efficient and just as helpful as he had promised.

In truth, I welcomed handing off Wrigley's fate to someone else. If Wrigley died during surgery at least we'd given him a chance. I didn't quite understand or share Lisa's faith in the surgery, but the decision was very important to her. I wasn't sure where my heart lay because I not only didn't want him to suffer any longer, I didn't want the burden of his intense care needs any longer either.

This time as Lisa, Wrigley and I waited in the small conference room, we could hear a vet speaking with another pet owner through the wall.

"Are you hearing this?" Lisa asked me. "It's breaking my heart. It makes me want to give her the money."

The woman in the room next to us was crying. Her pet required life saving surgery. She didn't have the money. Neither did we, but it wasn't stopping us. The MRI and the surgery cost would total $7649.00. Wrigley was ten months old. His care was averaging $1750.00 a month.

"We can give her one of our credit cards. I'll tell her there's a cute blonde over here, and you wanted to know if she'd like to join us in our misery," I suggested.

"You're not funny, Paul," she said. "Well, maybe you're a little funny." A smile snuck across her face.

Just then, Dr. Knoeckel walked in. Wrigley shifted his face to the left to watch him. "There are a few things we need to go over." His demeanor was different than during our two previous meetings. His calm aura was one of intensity and purpose.

"I'm estimating his surgery will last three and a half hours. Once we're in, we'll send a fragment of the tumor pressing on his spine to the lab. If it's cancer, it may have spread to other areas in his body. If that's the case, you'll have to make a decision while he's on the table. I'll call you if that happens, so you'll need to be available during the time of his surgery. Because of the complexity of this procedure, it's imperative his central nervous system not be disturbed, but if it is, he could become paralyzed on the table, and once again, you'll have to make a decision," Dr. Knoeckel told us.

Lisa and I agreed that if any of those complications occurred, we'd let Wrigley go.

"Everyone upstairs is ready. Time for you to say goodbye to your boy here and let us get to work," Dr. Knoeckel said. "I'll call you when he wakes up."

"That's the man who is going to save your life Wrigley," I said.

I felt bad for the young technician whose job it was to retrieve Wrigley. Our puppy was on death's door, but he could still be stubborn. Wrigley wanted nothing to do with leaving us and refused to go with the tech.

Five minutes later two male attendants came in, picked Wrigley up, set him on a gurney and wheeled him down the long hallway.

Lisa and I watched Wrigley stare at us woefully as they pushed the gurney through the double doors. He let out a weak bark before disappearing from our view.

It reminded me of the goodbye bark he'd mustered for Riley before she died. My heart sank. Resolutely, I pushed the thought out of my mind.

Lisa had a mandatory manager's meeting at two-thirty that afternoon. She promised she'd leave at three-thirty whether the meeting was over or not. There were so many times when it was difficult for her to extricate herself from the hospital. Hers was a demanding job, physically and emotionally, making our personal situation even more difficult at times.

"I can't just leave a patient," she would tell me. "How would you like it if a nurse told you to wait for the next shift for something you desperately needed? It's not the kind of job I can just punch out and leave."

This time, Lisa stuck to her promise and made it home by four forty-five. I was impressed and glad she was home.

"What have you been up to in here?" She surveyed the work I'd done. The dining room table was now pushed in the far corner of the room. I had stacked the chairs on top, out of the way. In the middle of the room, a brand new Beautyrest twin mattress waited, still wrapped in plastic.

"Paul, why on earth is there a mattress in the dining room? Did Dr. Knoeckel or the hospital call? What do you want for dinner?"

Ah, the nice normal routine of three questions at once. Not only that, I'd seen all three cats that afternoon, and it wasn't because I'd opened a can of their food either.

"The mattress is for Wrigley," I said. "Who knows how long it'll be before he can get up on his sofa? He loved sleeping in our bed. Now he has his own. It'll be more comfortable than the dog bed. He'll be able to stretch out, like he does on his sofa."

"You're so cute sometimes. I hope you kept the receipt because there's no way our dog is going near that thing. Wrigley will be hiding under that furniture first. He's scared of anything new. Don't take the plastic off so we can return it. God knows we need the money."

I retreated upstairs to my office.

Within an hour Lisa appeared in the doorway. "I'm sorry for what I said about the mattress. You're sweet. I'll still bet you twenty bucks we return it." She offered her handshake to seal the bet.

"You couldn't just leave your apology alone, could you?" I grumbled. "If he's going to be laying around for twenty-two hours a day recovering, don't you think the mattress will be more beneficial than that clumpy dog bed?"

"We'll see." She smiled and squeezed my shoulders before heading down to fix dinner. We ate, watching the clock, but no call came.

After six-thirty rolled around, I said, "Let's just call and see if there is any news. No crime in that."

"They may have started late or Wrigley might be taking a long time to wake up from the anesthesia," Lisa supposed. "It's a good sign that Dr. Knoeckel didn't call earlier. That means the tumor wasn't cancerous."

At eight-thirty we knew exactly what we did at six-thirty: nothing.

"Is your cell phone charged? You gave them that number, right? Did you check your messages?" Lisa paced around the living room.

I answered once with a yes for all three questions.

Lisa paced into the library, checking our answering machine. It hadn't been turned on since the move because no one ever called our home number except telemarketers or worse, politicians.

I was resting on Wrigley's new mattress in the dining room staring at the chandelier when Lisa decided to call the animal hospital. "Turn your phone on speaker," I yelled. "I want to hear what they say."

She was on hold for ten minutes before someone picked up. "Mrs. Sullivan, I'm sorry, but only the night staff is here now. The records are closed. Dr. Knoeckel told me to apologize to you for not calling," I heard the woman tell her.

"What does that mean?" I asked, after Lisa hung up. "He's sorry he didn't call? Does he think we're just hanging out here, like this is just another evening for us? Something's fucked up and they're afraid to tell us," I decided.

"Paul, calm down. Dr. Knoeckel isn't Dr. Evil. I'm sure there's a reason we haven't heard anything, but I agree, it is strange that she didn't have any information. God, I have a new appreciation for people waiting at the hospital for their loved ones coming out of surgery. Some people get crazy wanting to know every detail. I know exactly how they feel now."

"This is a miserable way to experience empathy," I complained.

My cell phone rang at ten-ten PM. It was Dr. Knoeckel.

"Don't put it on speaker," Lisa said. "I can't bear to hear any more bad news. Just tell me what he said when you're off." She closeted herself behind the library doors.

"Hi Paul, it's Mike. Wrigley came through surgery. He's resting in stable condition, but extremely groggy. I believe I extracted all of the tumor. It wasn't cancerous. The surgery took a great deal longer than I'd anticipated. The preliminary scratch tests to his feet and limbs show he's not exhibiting any paralysis at this time. The real test happens when he revives, and we can see if he can stand and walk on his own," he said.

I was speechless. I was so used to bad news, I'd forgotten how to celebrate wonderful news.

Finally, I stuttered out, "That's awesome. Thank you so much. It's unbelievable. When can we see him?"

"He'll be under observation all night. We don't want him getting excited seeing you because it may cause him to move around. If he has a good night, plan on coming by around noon tomorrow."

"Great. When do you think he'll be able to come home?" I asked.

"Like I said, if he does well tonight, tomorrow at noon."

"We can see Wrigley at noon, and you think he can come home when? That was my question," I clarified.

Dr. Knoeckel repeated, "Tomorrow at noon, if all goes well tonight. Make sure you don't leave with him tomorrow without seeing me first."

Lisa was in the library with her head on the desk, her hands pressed over her ears. She read me perfectly when I opened the door. I wasn't hiding my joy. She jumped up. "He made it! Didn't he?" she screamed.

"He's alive! He's not paralyzed! And he's cancer-free. He's going to be fine." Tears rolled down my face.

Lisa and I hugged the breath out of each other for a full minute.

"I can't believe that dog. You're so right, he's a fighter." I picked Lisa up and swung her into the foyer.

"You want to know the biggest news? And I mean huge?" I jumped up and down, waving my arms in the air like I was at a concert. "Wrigley's coming home TOMORROW!" I shouted.

"Tomorrow? How can that be?"

Precious, Cassie and Zoe were all in the living room. They may have gathered to celebrate with us but it was more likely that they had convened because I had forgotten to feed them dinner. "If you feed the cats, I'll open a bottle of champagne," I said.

"I have to work tomorrow," she protested. "It's not fair. Promise you'll call the second you see him and tell me everything."

The cats meowed when Lisa opened the first can of their stinky food. "Give them the Bumble Bee tuna. We're celebrating!" I popped the cork from the bottle of champagne.

* * *

I arrived at South Paws at eleven-thirty, a half hour early, but didn't mind the wait. After they installed me in a room, the same young girl who had tried to walk Wrigley to his surgery poked her head in and asked, "Would you like to see Wrigley?"

Before I could answer, Wrigley's big black nose poked out from behind her leg. His skinny head followed. He looked a foot taller with his head standing high.

"Wrigley! He's standing. I can't believe you, buddy." I met him nose to nose in the middle of the room. "His tail is wagging!"

Wrigley swung his head around like Ray Charles when he sang one of his classic songs. He shifted from side to side, celebrating our reunion. He backed up, moved his head in a joyous circular motion and barked. I'd never heard him bark such a deep sound before.

"He's a different dog!" I wrapped my hands around him, interlocking my fingers under his chest. I wanted to pick him up and twirl him around like I'd done with Lisa the night before. I was embarrassed to find myself crying, but the technician joined in. It was a beautiful moment. I wish Lisa could have experienced it with us.

"He hasn't been able to wag his tail in over a month! I can't believe how much taller he is with his head up. It's like he's turned into a full grown Great Dane overnight."

The tech went down a list of discharge instructions. I didn't take my hands or eyes off of Wrigley. Twenty-four staples held his ten-inch incision together. It started behind the top of his neck and stopped where his shoulders started. His poor eyes still oozed. He'd lost eighteen pounds in the last four weeks and the mange had claimed a third of his tattered coat.

Nevertheless, he looked awesome to me. His sudden ability to walk was the closest thing to a miracle I've known.

"I love my job," the young attendant said. "Every once in a while I get to experience this. It's great. When I left last night at seven Wrigley was still in surgery. The surgical team closed him at nine-thirty. His surgery time may be a record here at seven and a half hours.

"First thing this morning I went to Wrigley's crate. He wasn't there. I started crying. I had a really good feeling he'd make it for some reason. I get that from certain animals. Then John, who monitors recoveries at night, told me Wrigley was outside peeing. He's a special boy and lucky to have you."

After I initialed the discharge instructions she handed me a bag of medications and other stuff Wrigley needed for his recovery. Before leaving, she leaned down and hugged Wrigley. "I'll never forget you.

You're a champ and a lucky dog to have a family who loves you so much."

She smiled at me. "You went the distance with him. You've done a wonderful thing."

I've heard of people becoming overwhelmed with emotion over a celebrity or meeting somebody famous and being unable to speak. That day I was unable to express my appreciation and respect for the work Dr. Knoeckel performed on Wrigley. I'm sure by my fifth "thank you" he was ready to run away from me.

"He did real well," Dr. Knoeckel said. "Remember to keep him quiet. You can already see he feels better. Notice his weight shift back to the left rear leg? He'll build that up over time. We'll meet again in a week." He crouched down to pet Wrigley goodbye. "Remember, keep him calm," he reminded me as we exited through the lobby.

Six days earlier Lisa and I had walked out of South Paws and the beautiful spring day had mocked us. That day, I walked out the same doors with Wrigley and my world, my universe, was in perfect synchronicity. It was an awesome feeling.

Wrigley no longer dragged his back left leg. On the way home, I caught a glimpse of him in the rear view mirror as he stood up to reposition himself. He had never stood up back there before.

I called Lisa on the way back home and shared every single detail of our joyous reunion.

"I wish I was there," she said. "I'm so happy. Dr. Knoeckel saved his life. That man was on a mission. I could tell when he met with us. I'm so glad we gave him the chance. Thank you, sweetie. I love you. Tell Wrigley I love him, too."

Lisa couldn't stand being at work knowing Wrigley was already home. She actually left on time again and made it home before dark. She had to walk right by the mattress wrapped in plastic sitting in the breezeway. She didn't say a word about it.

It wasn't a surprise when Cassie was the first feline to welcome Wrigley. She walked to him slowly, actually touching noses with him, before darting away. Precious walked by Wrigley on his way to dinner, giving him a brief look as he passed. I'm not sure Zoe noticed Wrigley had been gone.

Anybody driving by who happened to see Wrigley outside on our front lawn would still have thought he was a sickly, dying dog. He was bone thin, his neck had staples holding him together, he had clumps of fur missing and bloodshot, oozing eyes.

Lisa and I saw a rebounding puppy, full of puppy-possibility and surrounded by our love. He was a survivor. I think we were too.

Chapter 21

Growing Up

Wrigley became omnivorous. He ate everything we put in front of him with the exception of fish, which he simply did not like. In the first month after the neurosurgery he gained twenty-four pounds, making up for his lost weight and adding six more pounds.

His fur finally grew back, and his mange came under control. He had a beautiful, shiny coat. Most importantly, Wrigley could walk again. Keeping him quiet and calm was the difficult piece of his recovery. Wrigley's new mobility provided him a new lease on life.

Robin, our neighbor, was a known animal lover. She once rescued a neighbor's escaped cockatoo by swimming out to the middle of the lake and retrieving the distressed bird by breaststroking it back to shore while it balanced itself on her head.

Robin was a cat lover first and foremost. She had three felines, but still found room to hold a special place in her heart for Wrigley.

When she returned from a trip, she was driving by our house after his surgery. She spotted him, jumped out of her car and ran up to him, smothering our puppy with a loving hug.

Wrigley weaved up and down, going into his Ray Charles move, swaying his head back and forth and barking, his tail whipping rhythmically behind him.

"I didn't think I'd ever see you again, Wrigley." She kissed his snout, patting him all over.

"Neither did we," I said. "Pretty amazing, huh?" I had to calm Wrigley down and keep him from jumping on Robin.

Mike and Shelly lived two blocks away. They had two beautiful Ridgebacks, show quality. "I could have lost a week's pay betting against Wrigley," Mike said. "He looks amazing, Paul."

At every follow-up appointment, Dr. Knoeckel reinforced, reiterated, and repeated constantly, "Keep Wrigley calm and quiet."

Following that instruction was difficult. Wrigley wasn't a sickly Great Dane puppy anymore. He weighed 110 pounds and moved easily of his own accord. Mostly, he wanted to have fun running and playing with other dogs, but we couldn't allow it.

A metal plate, fastened by screws, fused Wrigley's neck and spine together. The plate left him vulnerable until he was fully healed. It brought joy to Lisa and me watching him flop around and chasing balls. He repeatedly dropped his rope at our feet, longing for a tug-of-war match, but such activities were forbidden.

Wrigley's eyes continued to be an issue. He'd been through enough, and we weren't in an emotional or financial position to pursue the eye surgery Dr. Shiller had recommended.

The ointment we applied eased his discomfort, but his lashes were still rubbing his eyes. Lisa theorized Wrigley's skittishness was connected to his impaired vision.

"He's comfortable with images of things he's familiar with, but he can't seem to make out new or different things. He always backs away from stuff. I'm telling you it's because he can't see because those lashes interfere with his vision." Her theory made sense.

On the last Friday in April, I took my usual walk with Wrigley around the lake in the morning. There wasn't any stopping or waiting for him anymore. He kept up or ran ahead if I threw a toy for him. As we approached the house on the way back, the noise from a commercial truck engine gasped to a stop in front of our house.

It was the tree guys ready to remove two tall skinny pines and several limbs that were hanging over the roof in the back. Six guys emerged from the one truck like a group of actors about to perform a skit.

Wrigley was now allowed to get up and down on his sofa by himself, because we convinced Dr. Knoeckel that keeping him off his favorite perch was too stressful for him. Wrigley had his favorite spot back and he loved it, but he wouldn't like it today with all the noise out back.

I met the foreman of the crew out front and explained I needed to have the noisy work completed first. I also asked him to move and use their wood chipper at the front of Robin's house, our neighbor. His eyes widened and then narrowed as if he was considering not whether I was crazy, but the depth of my craziness.

Maybe I shouldn't have explained my requests were for my recovering puppy, Wrigley. I don't speak fluent Spanish, but I understood enough to know I'd been called a few rude names and was the punch line of a joke about a man being married to a real bitch.

I didn't care, I just wanted Wrigley calm.

I should have canceled the work then and there, but Lisa was afraid to sleep in our bedroom, located on the top floor in the back of the house, because she was convinced a tree or limb was going to crash onto our bed and kill us.

"My friend Jennifer lived through hurricane Hugo in 1989, Paul. The wind almost pulled the roof off her house. I'm not sleeping under those death-limbs," she told me. The slightest inclement weather and Lisa headed to the guest room.

I turned on a classical music station, turned up the volume and put Riley's old bed in the library. I called Wrigley in, gave him a treat and closed the doors. He'd be fine in there until the noisy work was finished.

To show my appreciation to the crew for the extra effort they had to put in, even after being called nasty words, I put twelve kielbasa sausages on the grill and fed the crew.

They devoured their lunch in five minutes and headed back to their truck. I released Wrigley from the library after writing out the check. When I handed it to the foreman I heard a leaf blower start up out back.

"What's that?" I asked him.

"There was sawdust on the upper deck from the white oak. Chino's blowing it off. It'll only take a minute," he explained.

I ran back into the house. Wrigley was halfway up the stairs. He stopped when he saw me, tried to turn around, lost his footing and fell, completing a full somersault. He crashed at the bottom of the stairs.

His yelp cut straight through me.

Wrigley lay still only because I refused to allow him to get up. When I released him tentatively, he picked himself up and strolled over to the sofa. To be safe, I gave him a Tramadol tablet just in case he had any pain. It would help keep him quiet for a while too.

"It's not your fault, Paul," Lisa told me. "It's one of those things that happens, honey."

Luckily, Wrigley was more stunned than hurt by his tumble.

Three days passed with no sign Wrigley was any worse for the wear.

That following weekend while I was walking him, Wrigley saw some of his old friends come around the corner. Without warning, he ran across the street towards Breezy and Izzy, Mike's two dogs.

Izzy playfully crossed the neighbor's lawn with Wrigley in full pursuit. Despite Izzy's advantage, Wrigley caught up with her. His motion resembled that of a lumbering black bear and a bunny hopping. He wasn't graceful, but he had speed.

Once he reached his opponent, he swung his front right paw, accidentally nailing Izzy square on her head.

She barked, letting out a high-pitched yelp, startling even Wrigley for a second.

Izzy retreated, rejoining her companion Breezy by Mike's side.

Wrigley wasted no time bouncing back to me, still anxious to play. I grabbed his collar.

"He's never done that before. Sorry, Mike. Is Izzy alright?" I asked.

"She's gotten it a lot worse from Breezy. Don't worry about it. Damn though, you've got a horse on your hands!" Mike walked away with his pups close by his side, looking back at me and Wrigley every few seconds.

"Wrigley. No street." I commanded. "No street. Street bad."

Wrigley's left rear leg began dragging behind him a week after his fall down the stairs. His head began to droop a bit as well. A mass of fluid had formed over his neck, where his surgery had taken place.

Dr. Knoeckel wasn't too concerned at first. "Swelling is normal at the surgical site. Albeit, it is late in the game in his recovery to see any significant swelling now. Use warm compresses. Do it ten times a day for at least twenty minutes. That should reduce the swelling."

Unfortunately, the swelling increased that week. The fluid under his neck grew to the size of a K-2 football by Saturday morning.

Dr. Knoeckel was out of town until Monday. The pocket of fluid was trapped under Wrigley's skin, sitting atop his neck, bouncing as he walked.

JoAnn, Dr. Shiller's assistant, squeezed us into their busy Saturday schedule.

"The fluid is symptomatic of an infection. I'm afraid something has come loose," Dr. Shiller said. "The symptoms he's showing are mimicking those he had with the spinal compression. I'm afraid this is serious." He advised us to take Wrigley back to see Dr. Knoeckel.

To reduce the pressure, Dr. Shiller used a syringe to draw fluid out. It was the same kind of needle he had used to draw Riley's belly fluid before her fatal diagnosis of peritonitis.

Wrigley's symptoms disappeared once the fluid was removed. He walked and behaved normally the rest of the day, but we still set up an appointment with Dr. Knoeckel for Tuesday.

That Sunday morning we stepped right back in time to a disastrous place.

When I came downstairs, Wrigley was despondent on his sofa. He looked terrible.

I tried to lift him off the sofa. He didn't offer me any help. I called for Lisa.

Wrigley was now 125 pounds. Because of my back, I couldn't lift him on my own, especially when he lay in a dead weight position. After help with the initial hoist, I could carry him.

Lisa held the front of his body while I moved behind. We carried him out the front. The storm door closed, hitting my funny bone and causing me to drop my half of Wrigley.

He yelped and passed out.

"Drag him," Lisa said. "He's worse than last time."

Thank God for church goers, because there wasn't any traffic that Sunday morning. We arrived at South Paws in twenty-five minutes, half the time it would normally take.

Lisa never uttered a word of protest or reprimand when I cruised through red lights or hit eighty-five mph on the Beltway.

We spent two hours that morning waiting at the animal hospital before speaking with the attending vet. I tuned out half of what she was telling us because I'd heard it all before.

"Wrigley's resting. Unfortunately, he's not doing well. His heart rate was elevated when he arrived. He's dehydrated too. His infection is troubling because he's been on some strong antibiotics. We think something's loose or has shifted in the surgical location. He needs to stay tonight and maybe longer. I spoke with Dr. Knoeckel. He's moved up your appointment to eight in the morning if you can get here," she said.

Lisa asked for clarification, "Eight, Tuesday?"

"No, tomorrow. Dr. Knoeckel's not on the schedule, but he's coming in for Wrigley," she said.

Monday morning I experienced a flashback to my elementary school years. The only difference was instead of the principal admonishing me, it was Dr. Knoeckel. Bottom line, Lisa and I were equally to blame for allowing Wrigley to participate in dangerous puppy play.

"Letting him play freely jeopardizes everything we've done to help him," Dr. Knoeckel told us. "You're not the first people who didn't follow discharge instructions of restraint, so don't beat yourselves up too badly."

Lisa and I hung our heads. Reflexively I looked at the clock on the wall, hoping the bell would ring so I could be dismissed.

"I'm confident the screws securing the plate are loose. I need to go back in and tighten them up. I underestimated Wrigley's intensity and desire to play. There is a chance he's caused some permanent nerve damage. When the fluid is gone and the screws are tightened, we'll find out. Any questions?"

I asked, "Is this going to cost as much as his last surgery?"

"I'm considering this a complication, related to his initial surgery. I've informed the hospital to bill his overnight and emergency care under the same consideration. I'm not billing you for my surgical time. The only cost to you will be the anesthesiologist's time and whatever surgical supplies are used. This will be a much quicker procedure than the last surgery," he said.

Lisa asked, "We were wondering if while he's under, would it be possible to perform the eye surgery he needs? Is that something that can arranged since he will already be under anesthesia?"

"Protocol rules against it, but his eyes are bad. Let me see if it can be coordinated. Either way, I'm proceeding with his surgery tomorrow. We'll keep him overnight again. He'll be comfortable, and we'll keep his IVs flowing. If all goes well, he should be able to go home tomorrow evening. I'll call you tonight about the eye surgery," he said.

When we walked around the lake that evening, Zoe followed us from a distance. It was strange not having a dog with us. We sat down at the bench on our way back, gazing out at the water.

Lisa asked me, "Do you think Wrigley will ever have a normal life?"

I laughed. "Lisa, the apropos question is, 'Will *we* ever have a normal life with Wrigley?'"

Dr. Knoeckel's assistant called us at nine-thirty that evening.

"Wrigley's doing much better. He ate some kibble. He's not dehydrated any longer. Dr. Blumenthal agreed to come in tomorrow and perform Wrigley's eye surgery. Both doctors will call to update you after their respective surgeries. You'll need to pay $1375.00 for the eye surgery when you come in.

"Wrigley looks much better than yesterday. Have a good night."

Thankfully, both of Wrigley's procedures went well. Lisa had taken the day off, hoping we'd be bringing him home. She didn't want to miss another post-crisis reunion.

Unfortunately, Dr. Knoeckel wanted another overnight. "You can pick him up at three tomorrow. He'll be waiting for you. It's obvious he misses you both."

I had not been out with my friends, other than maybe meeting for a quick lunch, in over five months. I needed a break desperately and with Wrigley in the hospital for another day, I had a chance to get away from it all.

I gathered three friends on short notice for nine holes of golf. I felt free knowing Wrigley was fine and wasn't coming home until the next day. We played nine holes and drank as many beers. My night out with the guys ran into the early morning.

A friend dropped me back at the house at two-thirty AM. I was pretty sure I left my car at the course.

I undressed and climbed into bed with Lisa.

"God, you reek! Did you marinate yourself in alcohol?" she muttered in annoyance. "Please tell me you didn't drive home in your state."

"I didn't drive home in Virginia, occifer," I said with a laugh. "Bill did. He has a seven o'clock meeting. He was our designated driver. He took one for the boys. He stopped drinking at midnight."

"Comforting, Paul. Great plan. Listen, I have to get up in two hours. Please don't turn on the TV and if you're going to snore, leave now." She rolled over on her side. I was feeling quite amorous.

I had the good judgment not to drive, but my smarts failed me now. I pressed my naked body against Lisa.

"Did you make a hole-in-one today?" she asked me, the tone of her voice sounding a warning.

"No."

My fuzzy brain didn't have time to wonder what she was talking about before she said, "You aren't going to be that lucky now either, especially after drinking so much."

The next thing I remembered was my phone ringing. It was super bright inside the bedroom, despite the blinds being closed tightly.

When I answered, it was Lisa. She was at work.

"I'm going to meet you at South Paws. I got off work early. Are you on your way?" she asked.

"What time is it?" I adjusted my eyes, trying to see the clock radio on the nightstand.

"Two-thirty. Why? Where are you?"

"Just leaving, sweetie. I'll see you there." I jumped up, got dressed, grabbed a baseball cap and two Ritalin before heading out the door.

Lisa was waiting for me in a small conference room on the second floor of the hospital.

When I walked in, she shook her head at me.

"I woke you up, didn't I?"

"Possibly." Lying was pointless. She knew.

My mouth was the Sahara desert, my head hurt and my own breath was nearly choking me. I was paying the price for jamming five months of missed partying into one long night.

Adding to my pain, Dr. Knoeckel read Lisa and me the riot act one more time before we got to see Wrigley.

"No horseplay for four weeks. No exceptions. Understood?"

We promised him. He left the room and returned with our proud Great Dane puppy, Wrigley.

We could see his eyes clearly for the first time. They were brown. Despite being covered in post-surgical ointment, they looked one hundred percent better already. Without bloodshot and oozing eyes, Wrigley somehow looked taller. He was more attentive with his eyes open and his neck upright. The fur on his neck was gone again and a new row of staples lined his latest incision, but he didn't seem worse for the wear.

It had been almost three days since we'd seen him. He looked better than I felt.

Dr. Blumenthal, the ophthalmic surgeon, told us she would normally have waited to do the procedure until after Wrigley was full grown. There was a chance he would regrow or sprout new lashes because he had not yet reached full size. She had only agreed to proceed with his surgery because his condition was so severe.

Lisa and I had no idea he was so close to losing his sight. If he hadn't fallen and required the follow-up spinal surgery, he may have become blind. Nothing happened by design or plan with Wrigley. Yet he kept moving forward, pressing on, better than before and never looking back.

Lisa and I followed the discharge and recovery instructions to a fault. Our reward was a thriving puppy.

Four weeks later, Dr. Knoeckel gave Wrigley the green light to play without restraint.

He had finally fully recovered.

Great Danes aren't considered fully grown until twenty-four months. Wrigley wasn't a monster-sized Great Dane, but he weighed 143 pounds at eleven months. He was lean and all muscle. He walked with an awkward gait, but had a spring in his step and nothing slowed him down.

The slight hump in his back that formed after his vaccination shot didn't go away.

Wrigley regained rock star status in the neighborhood, but one thing changed. Wrigley, or Big Wrig, as my younger brother Mark called him, was now the biggest boy on the block. Other dogs took notice and kept their distance when Wrigley wanted to play. His knack for clobbering dogs while he ran alongside them was nothing but play for Wrigley, but the other animals and their owners often didn't see it that way.

We restrained him with a harness, but he still jumped up and down, all four paws off the ground, when other dogs approached. We held him back.

We had come from caring for a frail, handicapped pup to trying to manage a fun-loving, strong-willed, large Great Dane puppy. I was thrilled.

Wrigley had finally evolved into the dog I'd waited for all those years. His scars reminded me how far he'd come and how well he was doing. Things settled into a pleasant routine for us. If this was normal, I preferred it.

Chapter 22

Saving our Lives

In less than a month, Wrigley was going to be one year old. That wasn't a milestone in most dogs' lives, but we considered it a miracle for our puppy. Lisa, Wrigley and I walked down the path past the bench to an opening in the woods. The wind was howling from the unexpected front moving in from the Midwest.

We watched the tall oaks and birch trees sway back and forth while leaves flew wildly in circles in the air.

"You want to go down Mystery Road, Wrigley?" I asked him.

"Mystery Road" was a path created by the neighbors across the lake. Their riding mowers had cleared the brush down a hill and into the woods. Half the time we walked it we spotted deer or a fox. Wrigley loved running down the trail, exploring the terrain in hopes of "catching" some wildlife. He never came close, but gave admirable effort in chase several times.

When he was done hunting, he'd jump up and down, turning in circles with excitement. It didn't appear to matter to him if he caught anything.

Lisa and I started down the hill into the woods.

Wrigley uncharacteristically stayed at the top of the path, anxiously turning and making half grunt, half bark noises at us.

"What's up, Wiggles?" I had to raise my voice over the noisy wind.

Wrigley backed up, then moved ten feet down the path, only to turn around and repeat his anxious dance from the trailhead.

"That's weird," Lisa said. "We usually have to hold him back from running out of sight when we come down here."

"Maybe the wind is scaring him. You know how he freaks with weird noises."

Lisa looked up at the dark clouds overhead. "Yeah, looks like it's about to rain, anyway. Let's go back."

We turned, headed back up the trail and met Wrigley at the top of the hill. He had calmed down as soon as we reached him, and he happily led the way toward the house. He stayed close, making sure we were following him.

We hadn't gone more than a few yards from the trailhead when we heard a loud blast, similar to a sonic boom. Behind us, a magnificent oak tree with a circumference of at least ten feet snapped in two. Debris flew everywhere. The noise from the blast stunned us for a moment.

We stared back down Mystery Road. One colossal limb lay across the path only a few feet from where we would have been standing if Wrigley hadn't turned us around a minute earlier.

"Holy shit! That's unbelievable," I said in awe. "Did you hear how loud that was?"

Lisa stared at the fallen tree in amazement.

"We could have been killed by that thing. Let's get out of here and get inside," she urged.

Wrigley was sitting down at our feet, something he never did when we were out for a walk. Then it hit me. He knew. He sensed, heard or felt the coming lightning strike. It was the only reason I could come up with for him refusing to lead or join us down "Mystery Road."

"Wrigley. You saved us, buddy. You funny puppy. How'd you know?"

Lisa crouched down on her knees, giving Wrigley a huge thank you hug.

"I've always known you were brought into our lives for a reason, Wrigley," she told him.

He jumped up, pushed his big head into Lisa's face and licked it while she was praising him.

"Gross, Wrigley! His tongue touched mine, Paul," she screeched.

I laughed. "Hey Lisa, I've been meaning to bring up your terrible doggy-breath. Now that I know how you got it, the focus of that discussion has to change." I wanted to say more, but I was laughing too hard.

"Oh, stop it," she complained, trying to spit out the contaminated saliva from her mouth.

Wrigley started running back toward the house without us.

"He's like Lassie, you think the rescue is complete, but danger still lies ahead." I grabbed Lisa's hand, while picking up our pace. "Seriously, based on his recent premonition, we'd better get our butts out of here and follow him."

The storm that followed that afternoon was wicked, with intense thunder and lightning. It was the kind of weather that made me happy to be safely inside. It also reminded me of how fragile life is and how easily things can change with no warning.

That night, after the storm had passed, Lisa and I sat out on the deck. I'd brought Wrigley's bed out and placed it near our chairs. He lay on it snoring.

"I've got a question. It involves math," I told Lisa.

"I'm about as good at math as you, Paul. Don't expect much help from me."

"We saved Wrigley three times from death, and he's now saved us once. Does that count as two saves for him, because we're two people?"

"You're silly," Lisa told me. "I will give odds on the probability he knew that tree was coming down though. One hundred percent, in my mind. I'm serious. He knew something was about to happen. He saved us."

"I think you're right. But honestly, I think he has been working on saving us long before that tree came down today. He's a funny boy. I never imagined the path he *refused* to take us down would be the one that possibly saved our lives. Maybe we should put Wrigley's photo next to the word 'ironic' in Wikipedia," I suggested.

"Funny, I think his picture would be best suited next to the phrase 'unconditional love,'" Lisa said, reaching for my hand and holding it gently.

"Maybe all three of our faces could be on that one." I smiled at her.

"You're cute." She leaned over and kissed me. "I'm going up to change and get dinner ready. You coming?"

"Yep. In a few minutes," I told her.

"If I peel the potatoes, will you make your mashies with the real butter? I feel like being bad tonight," Lisa said.

"Wow, married six years and 'being bad' is now defined as slipping butter into potatoes. Life changes fast, doesn't it?"

"I can be bad in other ways too, Paul."

"Hmm. That sounds promising."

"Bring Wrigley up, will you? It's time for his dinner too." She sauntered away towards the door.

"I will when he wakes up, which will probably be the second he hears the breezeway door shut and realizes you're inside."

She paused and looked back at Wrigley and me. "You want to know what's ironic, Paul? Even when you don't have to, you find a way to spend time with him. I believe you've come to not only accept, but actually enjoy, waiting for Wrigley."

"Reading me like an open book, aren't you?"

Wrigley opened his eyes, and we both watched Lisa walk up the deck steps, through the breezeway, and into the house.

"We've been figured out, big boy," I told him. "Being known is like having mashed potatoes and gravy with dinner. Comfort food, good times. Feels nice. Come on Wiggles, let's go eat."

I rested my hand on the back of Wrigley's neck, letting him know it was time to go. We walked up the steps and inside together.

Lisa gave him a quick hug and kiss on his head as he passed her, heading to his favorite spot on the sofa.

"Wrigley, Lisa put your food out, buddy. You're not hungry?" I asked him.

"You know you talk to him like he's a person," Lisa said with a sweet smile.

"And your point is?"

"You guys are real buddies. He looks like he might know what you're saying half the time."

"Yeah, I wonder if he knows what I'm thinking right now," I said, taking Lisa and giving her a warm hug.

"I wish I had that insight," she responded.

"I think we both know you do right now." I gave her a soft kiss.

"Yeah, well you're not always this easy to figure out, Paul. You and Wrigley are too much alike. You're both simple in some ways, but twice as complicated in others," she said, shaking her head.

"What fun would that be if you knew everything before it happened? Life would be pretty boring, don't you think?"

"I wouldn't mind knowing if a tree was about to fall on my head. That would be nice."

"Isn't that why we call it 'Mystery Road?' If you think about it, we've been walking an uncharted path ever since Wrigley came into our lives."

"We've been doing that since we met," Lisa corrected me. "Paul, would you do it again? Would you walk down the aisle and take me as your wife today, knowing we won't have children of our own?"

Her eyes began to flood with tears. She was seriously asking me. I wondered how she could have any doubt.

"Nothing prepared me for you, Lisa. That's why every day we spend together feels new. We've definitely been through some tough patches. Don't you realize I'd have never gotten through them if it wasn't you by my side? I know we've swayed apart for periods, and those were always the most difficult times for me. There was a sense of loneliness when you were so close, but you felt so far away. You know the reason Wrigley's staring at us right now? He's probably wondering why you're crying because he's doing just fine. I think we've learned together there are never any guarantees, except knowing how we feel in the moment. That's the only real thing that exists, positively, and then that goes away; lasting as only a memory. I don't have any delusions, Lisa. Our life together will probably continue to be unpredictable, always surprising and I'm sure at times, painful. I'm confident the odds are in our favor though. You know why? Because of our love for each other and for Wrigley. We'll always find a way to balance things. I could never quit on you. I love you and I love me too much to do that.

"I think back on all the time I spent waiting for Wrigley. Maybe he's staring at us right now because he's wondering how long it's going to take for me to tell you how much I love you and need you. Everything we've gone through with him reminds me every day why I chose you."

I dropped down on my right knee, looking deep into Lisa's eyes, "Would you give me the honor, once more?"

"Don't be silly," she said, jumping on me, knocking me over and kissing me. "Of course I will. Because I'm crazy, just like you!"

Wrigley jumped off the sofa. He ran over to us, threw his head around in half circles and started barking.

"Wrigley, save me from this man," Lisa said laughing. "He's stealing my heart again!"

About the Author

My wife, Lisa, and I live with Wrigley, our proud Great Dane, Callie our rescued Lab and the latest addition to our family, Brody, a mischievous kitten that has "rocked" Wrigley's world in a wonderfully playful way. We currently live in Northern Virginia. My undergraduate degree is from George Mason University, BS, Public Administration, and I completed my graduate program at Virginia Commonwealth University in Richmond, with an MSW, Clinical Social Work, specializing in mental health. I've worked as a certified bereavement facilitator for hospice, leading support groups and providing individual counseling. This is my first published work. Currently, I am spending my time promoting *Waiting for Wrigley*, and finishing the final edits on *Waiting for Wrigley, Too*.

Visit Paul and Wrigley at:
www.waitingforwrigley.com
or email:
waiting4wrigley@gmail.com

www.ingramcontent.com/pod-product-compliance
Lightning Source LLC
Chambersburg PA
CBHW031445040426
42444CB00007B/984